Preface

Language is a continuous process. It changes ..... passage of time. English has undergone dramatic changes since the time of Geoffrey Chaucer. As the world has become a global village, and science and technology have made quantum leaps, a number of phrases have also made their place safe in the English language. Thus, a reader should be aware of these phrases – and know how to use them correctly – in order to add spontaneity and flair to his or her English.

In this small book, I have presented those phrases that any English speaker really ought to have on his or her finger-tips. These phrases – diligently collected by me in my work as a newspaper editor over a period of more than 20 years – have been put in a concise and clear-cut manner, along with simple examples of usage. Though some of them may look beyond your ken and comprehension, they will surely add punch and power to your sentences and give you an edge when you use them in your spoken or written English. The book is handy, and can be carried by you much to your delight and enjoyment.

I express my gratitude to my former English teacher R.S. Rathore, I.A.S., Dr. B.P.R. Vithal, I.A.S. (and former Registrar of Osmania University), Siddharth Varadarajan (Associate Editor, The Hindu) and Archana and Sanjay Kapoor (Hardnews Media). Their love and sincerity I will always cherish till I pass on to the world of Eternal Life.

God bless all. Amen.

Joel Lyall
New Delhi

DICTIONARY OF MODERN PHRASES

With Meaning and Usage

JOEL LYALL
News Editor
Hardnews

UNICORN BOOKS

Publisher

UNICORN BOOKS

F-2/16, Ansari Road, Daryaganj, New Delhi-110002
☎ 011-23275434, 23262683, 23250704 • *Fax:* 011-23257790
E-mail: info@unicornbooks.in • *Website:* www.unicornbooks.in

Branch : Mumbai
23-25, Zaoba Wadi Thakurdwar, Mumbai-401002
☎ 022-22010941, 022-22053387
E-mail: rapidex@bom5.vsnl.net.in

ISBN 978-81-7806-123-8
Dictionary of Modern Phrases (English)

Edition: 2017

Printed at : *Unique Color Carton, Mayapuri, New Delhi-110064*

Dedicated to my family
and
the poor of India

Foreword

I am delighted that my former colleague, Mr. Joel Lyall, is publishing a book on phrases. Mr. Lyall has an encyclopaedic knowledge of the English language. Not only does he have the eagle's eye of a good editor but also an understanding of the English language that is rare to find.

Mr. Lyall was my valued colleague in The Times of India. Day in and day out for 365 days in a year, he would produce the editorial page and other pages of The Times of India. As the Editorial Page Editor, I could go home every evening without worrying about the quality of the page that would be printed that night and read next morning. This was because I could trust the professionalism of Mr. Lyall who made sure that an errorless page went to the press.

What made Mr. Lyall unique in New Delhi's media world was his authoritative grasp of the English language. Not only does he have a good command over English grammar and syntax, but also on phrases and metaphors that are the stock-in-trade of good journalism.

This book of phrases can be read with great profit both by students and those who wish to improve their English. English is today just another Indian language. Hence improving our understanding of English can help us communicate better.

Many of the phrases explained here are used by most of us as part of normal conversation and often we misuse them. For both those who use and misuse these phrases an understanding of what they actually mean would be valuable in improving their command of the English language.

I hope Mr. Lyall will find readers across the length and breadth of India and all over the world, for English language is a global language.

—**Dr. Sanjaya Baru**
Media Advisor to PM

Hold in abeyance = *in suspension;* Hold the results in abeyance till further notice.

Abide by = *follow;* Always abide by the rules.

Set ablaze = *burn;* The house was set ablaze.

Abound with = *found in large numbers;* The river abounds with fishes.

About turn = *do the opposite;* The government made an about turn in its policy.

Keep abreast of = *up to date with new ideas;* We should keep abreast of technology.

Absolve of = *free from blame;* The judge absolved him of all crimes.

Abubble with = *full of excitement;* We are abubble with this new idea.

Abuzz with = *filled with sound;* The dark room was abuzz with flies.

Acceptable to = *suitable;* The idea is acceptable to me.

Access to = *the means to approach;* I have access to the teacher.

Accord with = *agree;* We are in accord with you.

Of one's own accord = *voluntarily;* He retired of his own accord.

According to = *as stated by;* We work according to a plan.

By all accounts = *as one has heard or read;* By all accounts he is a good boy.

Call someone to account = *make someone to explain a mistake;* I will call him to account for this bad work.

Give a good account of oneself = *give good impression;* He gave a good account of himself in the examination.

Keep an account of = *keep record;* Keep an account of your work.

On no account = *in no way;* On no account will I keep you away.

Of no account = *useless;* He is a man of no account.

Settle accounts with = *take revenge;* They will settle accounts with their enemies.

Take account of = *consider;* Take account of all other options.

Account for = *give reason;* You should account for your failure.

Accountable to = *responsible;* All human beings are accountable to God.

Accredited with = *to praise for something;* Cleopatra is accredited with being one of the most beautiful women.

Accuse of = *charge with crime;* He is accused of theft.

Ace out = *remove;* It is not good to ace a poor man out of his job.

Hold all the aces = *have all advantages;*   A man can never hold all the aces.

Acquit of = *free from charge;*   The magistrate acquitted him of murder.

Act out of = *be motivated by;*   Never act out of greed.

Act of God = *by natural forces;*   The Gujarat earthquake was an act of God.

Get one's act together = *prepare oneself to work effectively;*   Let us get our act together to pass the examination.

Act on = *work on;*   I act on your advice.

Act up = *fail to work;*   The machine is acting up.

In action = *engaged in work;*   I saw Wasim Akram in action.

Man of action = *man who works;*   Gandhiji was a man of action.

Out of action = *not working;*   The engine is out of action.

Achilles' heel = *weakness;*   Greed is the Achilles' heel of his character.

Put into action = *carry out;*   Put your ideas into action.

A faithful Adam = *old servant;*   He is my faithful Adam.

Adam's profession = *agriculture;*   Most of the villagers are in Adam's profession.

Adonis = *beautiful boy;*   He is an Adonis.

To address = *to solve;*   We should address the problem.

Adapt to = *become adjusted;*   We all should adapt to new changes.

Adapt from = *taken;*   The movie was adapted from a Dickens novel.

Adept at = *skilled, expert;*   My friend is adept at solving these puzzles.

Admit of = *chance or possibility;*   Your carelessness admits of no excuse.

Ad nauseam = *again and again;*   This has been told ad nauseam.

In advance = *before time;*   You should book your ticket in advance.

Take advantage of = *misuse, exploit;*   Don't take advantage of his poverty.

In the affirmative = *agree to request;*   He answered in the affirmative.

All agog = *very keen;*   I am all agog to see you.

Ahead of = *before;*   I go ahead of you.

Ahead of one's time = *advanced, modern outlook;*   King Ashoka was ahead of his time.

Aim at = *directed;*   The advertisement is aimed at middle classes.

Aid package = *help;*   The government gives aid package to poor societies.

In the air = *present;*   Tom sensed danger in the air.

On air = *broadcast on radio/TV;*   The speech of the leader will be on air tomorrow.

Airtight = *very strong;*   The Australian hockey team has an airtight defence.

Airy-fairy = *foolish;*   Be practical. Don't believe in airy-fairy romances.

On the alert = *careful;*   The armed forces are on the alert.

Alarm bell = *warning of danger;* The blast has set alarm bells ringing all over the world.

Alarmist policy = *policy causing worry;* The US believes in alarmist policy.

Alight on = *find, notice;* My eyes alighted on this old picture.

Alive to = *know, aware of ;* The modern generation is alive to new technology.

Alive with = *full of ;* The rivers and ponds are alive with ducks and birds.

Alive and kicking = *very active;* The resistance is alive and kicking.

All over = *everywhere;* The papers were scattered all over the place.

All-round = *complete;* We believe in all-round development of the country.

All the way = *without condition;* I will support you all the way.

In all = *in total number;* We get Rs.500 in all.

All-powerful = *complete;* Hilter was an all-powerful dictator.

All-purpose = *of many uses;* This is an all-purpose tent.

Along with = *in company;* I was going along with them.

Be along = *arrive;* They will be along here soon.

Alter ego = *a close friend;* He is my alter ego.

Alumna = *a female ex-student of a college;* She is a Miranda alumna.

Alumnus = *a male ex-pupil of a college;* He is an alumnus of Cambridge University.

Make amends for = *correct;*   Make amends for your past mistakes.

Amount to = *come to;*   Our loss will amount to Rs.1,000.

Anchorman = *important man, presenter of news, shows;*   He is an anchorman of the BBC.

Anchor to = *based on;*   The government policy is anchored to reality.

The angel in the house = *a devoted woman;*   My mother is the angel in the house.

On the side of angels = *join what is right;*   Don't destroy forests. We are on the side of angels.

Angle for = *seek to get;*   I am angling for this post.

Animal spirit = *natural joy;*   She is full of animal spirits.

Angelic smile = *like an angel;*   You have an angelic smile on your face.

Answerable to = *responsible to report;*   A worker is answerable to his manager.

Answerable for = *responsible for;*   We are answerable for our mistakes.

Appetite for = *liking;*   China has no appetite for sanctions against Iran.

Have ants in one's pant = *restless;*   The boy has ants in his pants.

Make an appearance = *attend briefly;*   The actor made an appearance at the show.

By all appearances = *as far as seen;*   By all appearances, he was a nice man.

Appearance money = *money paid for appearance;* The club paid Rs.10 lakh appearance money to Ronaldo.

Apples and oranges = *two opposite things;* Terrorism and peace are apples and oranges.

A rotten apple = *corrupt person;* He is a rotten apple.

Upset the apple cart = *disturb the plan;* The Democrats upset the Republican apple cart.

Apropos of = *with reference to ;* Apropos of your letter, we send you this file.

Arch-enemy = *great enemy;* Osama is the US's arch-enemy.

Architect of = *man who is responsible;* Sachin was the architect of India's victory.

Argue out = *convince;* The teacher tried to argue the students out of it.

The long arms of = *power;* Nothing is beyond the long arms of the law.

An army of = *a large number of people;* There was an army of reporters.

Up in arms = *protest;* People are up in arms against the new rules.

An array = *many;* We have an array of friends.

Arrow-straight = *absolutely straight;* Please go arrow-straight.

As for = *with regard to;* As for you, you are a nice guy.

Be asking for trouble = *behaviour that results in trouble;* Don't do that. You'll be asking for trouble.

A big ask = *difficult demand;* You want a BMW car? It is a big ask.

For the asking = *something one can have easily;* You can have this for the asking.

Look askance at = *look suspiciously;* He looks askance at me.

Autumn of life = *old age;* You have reached the autumn of your life.

Attend with = *have;* Your journey is attended with danger.

Avail of = *take advantage;* We must avail of every opportunity.

Of little avail = *not very useful;* Your advice was of little avail.

To little avail = *with little success;* I worked hard but to little avail.

Avalanche of = *great quantity;* The work received an avalanche of criticism.

Averse to = *have great dislike;* Some people are averse to criticism.

Aware of = *know;* I am aware of the dangers.

Awe-inspiring = *very impressive;* Dickens wrote awe-inspiring novels.

Astronomical price = *very high;* The price of gold is astronomical.

Aggressive and astute = *persuasive;* He is an aggressive and astute salesman.

Pump up adrenaline = *inspire;* A good environment will pump up your adrenaline.

B

One's baby = *responsibility;* I will not do this work. It is not my baby.

Baby-faced = *having a baby-like face;* He is a baby-faced boy.

Bachelor girl = *unmarried young woman;* She is a bachelor girl.

At someone's back = *in support of;* My manager is at my back.

Back and forth = *to and fro;* He is walking back and forth.

At the back of someone's mind = *present;* The idea was at the back of my mind.

Back the wrong horse = *wrong choice;* Never back the wrong horse.

Put one's back into = *work with vigour;* We should put our back into our work.

Back down = *withdraw;* He backed down from his promise.

Back out = *withdraw commitment;* The company backed out of the agreement.

Back breaking = *tiring;* This is a back breaking job.

Back burner = *postpone;* The government has put this issue on the back burner.

Backgrounder ■ *information;* Give backgrounder of the company.

Backfire = *have opposite effect;* The plan will backfire on you.

Public backlash = *strong public reaction;* There was a public backlash against reservation.

Back room = *place of secret work;* Weapon scientists are back-room boys.

Backstairs deal = *secret deal;* Good people never make backstairs deals with businessmen.

Backtrack = *change;* Students backtracked on their demand, and joined classes.

Economic backwater = *area requiring progress;* Many villages are still in economic backwater.

Bad faith = *deceive;* The greedy man acted in bad faith.

Bag of nerves = *timid and tense;* She is a bag of nerves.

In the bag = *almost secured;* The election victory is in the bag.

Bail someone out = *release from difficulty;* I can bail you out.

In the balance = *uncertain;* My future hangs in the balance.

On balance = *after all considerations;* On balance he looked very happy.

Strike a balance = *compromise;* The party struck a balance with its critics.

Off balance = *unsteady;* The child is off balance and may fall.

Balancing act = *keep balance in different situations;* A leader requires a balancing act to maintain peace in party.

The ball is in your court = *now your turn;* The ball is in your court. You take the action.

Ballooning prices = *very high;* Nobody can afford these ballooning prices.

Balmy days = *pleasant;* How one can forget the balmy days of childhood?

Ballyhoo = *great publicity, fuss;* Despite the ballyhoo, the show proved a flop.

Out of the bandbox = *neat appearance;* You are coming out of the bandbox.

Bang on target = *successful;* The player was bang on target, and scored a goal.

Go with a bang = *be successful;* The team went with a bang, and won the match.

Bank on = *depend;* We can bank on our faithful friend.

Bankroll = *support;* The U.N. will bankroll this project.

Barefaced liar = *shameless;* He is a barefaced liar.

Barmy decision = *foolish;* The company took a barmy decision.

Barnstorming speech = *very successful;* He delivered a barnstorming speech.

A barrage of questions = *many;* We asked a barrage of questions.

Bated breath = *keenly, anxious;*   I was waiting with bated breath to see you.

Have a bash at = *attempt;*   A poor worker can have a bash at anything.

Baptism of fire = *difficult experience;*   The Jamshedpur steel mill was Tata's baptism of fire.

Bay for blood = *ask for punishment;*   Bush is baying for Saddam's blood.

Keep at bay = *keep at distance;*   Keep him at bay.

On the beat = *on duty;*   The policeman is on the beat.

At one's beck and call = *ready to help;*   I am at your beck and call.

Become of = *happen to;*   What will become of you?

Becoming dress = *nice clothings;*   She came in a becoming dress.

Bedlam = *confusion;*   There was bedlam in parliament.

Beef up = *strengthen;*   The team should beef up its performance.

Beefy body = *muscular;*   He has a beefy body.

Beg the question = *invite question;*   A new theory begs the question.

Bell the cat = *tackle danger;*   Who is ready to bell the cat?

Benchmark = *standard;*   None can challenge the benchmark of our product.

Bend one's knees = *submit;*   India can never bend its knees to any power.

The benefit of the doubt = *concession;* Umpires give the benefit of the doubt to the batsman.

Go berserk = *out of control;* The mob went berserk and attacked the police.

Beside the point = *irrelevant;* What you say is beside the point.

Get the better of = *defeat;* We got the better of our opponents.

Bid for = *attempt to achieve;* He is bidding for a place in the team.

Big stick = *use force;* The US uses a big stick to intimidate small countries.

Big time = *high level in a career;* Amitabh Bachchan has made it big time in Bollywood.

News blackout = *suppression;* There was a complete news blackout during Hitler's regime in Germany.

Draw a blank = *get no success;* The police went to search him out, but drew a blank.

Blanket ban = *complete;* There should be a blanket ban on injurious products.

Blaze a trail = *first to do a new thing;* J.D.Tata blazed a trail in many fields.

Play a blinder = *play excellently;* Ronaldo played a blinder against Germany.

Blitz = *attack and defeat;* Australia blitzed the West Indies in the ODI.

Blockbuster = *a great success;* 'Great expectations' was a blockbuster.

Taste blood = *get early success;* The team has tasted blood, and will go on to win the trophy.

Blue ribbon = *cosy, good quality;* The boy wants a blue ribbon job.

Body language = *movements showing feelings;* He expressed his feelings through his body language.

Boil down = *come to, amount to ;* The dealings boil down to money and cash.

To boot = *in addition;* You will get a luxurious house, and a garden to boot.

Bow out = *withdraw;* He has bowed out of business.

Brain-teaser = *amusing problem;* Some computer games are brain-teasers.

Brass tacks = *consider basic facts;* Don't speak nonsense. Get down to the brass tacks.

Bottom line = *most important point;* The bottom line is that we are earning profit.

Breathe fire and brimstone = *very angry;* He is breathing fire and brimstone.

Booming economy = *strong;* Japan has a booming economy.

Body blow = *setback;* New restrictions will be a body blow for industries.

Bleeding wound = *weak point, place;* Corrruption is a bleeding wound in our economy.

On the boil = *angry;* Students are on the boil over the issue of reservation.

Brand leader = *the best or the best selling;* Bill Gates is the brand leader of the computer industry.

Blow the chance = *misuse, waste;* Never blow a good chance.

Blow the whistle = *inform;* The boy saw the thief and blew the whistle.

Big breaking = *good, sensational;* It was a big breaking news.

A big draw = *popular, famous;* This new car is a big draw.

Breeding ground = *base, main point;* Pakistan is a breeding ground of terrorism.

Blank out = *reject;* Ganguly has been blanked out of team.

Breathe down the neck = *follow closely;* Bush is breathing down the neck of Iran.

Central banker = *main supporter;* According to the US, Tehran is the central banker of terrorism.

Blast one's way = *enter by force;* The US is trying to blast its way in all countries.

Build bridges = *build friendly relations;* They are building bridges with his critics.

Bog down = *stuck up, halt, stop;* Talks between the UN and Iran have bogged down on the nuclear issue.

Blow-by-blow = *describe events as they happen;* A TV reporter gives a blow-by-blow account of events.

Bitten by bug = *obsessive interest;* He is bitten by the editing bug.

Bonanza time = *time to make profit;* Diwali is bonanza time for businessmen.

Under the banner = *a part of a group;*   The company works without the support of big banners.

Brim with ideas = *full of;*   A good writer brims with new ideas.

On the back foot = *defensive;*   The reservation issue has put the government on the back foot.

Butterfly executive = *move from job to job;*   He is a butterfly executive.

Brush with = *encounter;*   I had a brush with a leopard in the jungle.

Calling = *profession;*   Teaching is his calling.

Calling card = *visiting card;*   This is my calling card.

Call curtains = *ban, stop;*   The government calls curtains on this movie.

In camera = *in private;*   The case was heard in camera.

Call the shots = *powerful thing, force;*   In the present age, it is money that calls the shots.

Camp follower = *a person of a group;*   John is a communist camp follower.

Seasoned campaigner = *expert and experienced;*   Sourav is a seasoned campaigner and should be included in the team.

Make capital out of = *use to advantage;*   The BJP made capital out of the scandal.

On the cards = *possible;*   The meeting is on the cards.

Cardinal point = *chief quality;*   Honesty is the cardinal point of his life.

Carping criticism = *continuous;*   He is making carping criticism against me.

Carpet bombing = *intensive;*   There was carpet bombing in Iraq.

Carpet knight = *avoid work but enjoy leisure;* There are many carpet knights in politics.

Carte blanche = *full freedom;* You are given carte blanche.

Carve out = *get with difficulty;* After all, he carved out his career.

A cascade = *a great amount;* There was a cascade of advertisements of this product.

Cash in = *exploit;* Advertisers cash in on a product's taste and appeal.

Cast cloud = *make bleak, dim;* Your poor performance may cast a cloud over your career.

Cataclysmic effect = *damaging, natural effects;* Felling of trees will have cataclysmic effect.

Catastrophic effect = *causing suffering;* World War II had catastrophic effects.

Catch on = *become popular;* The idea of fashion designing is fast catching on.

Catch-22 = *dilemma;* The US has reached a catch-22 situation on Iraq.

Cave in = *yield, submit;* The company caved in to his demands.

Cavil at = *object;* The customer cavils at his demand and price.

Cement the ties = *settle, establish;* The talks will cement the ties between the two countries.

Centre around = *focus on;* The discussions centred around education.

Centre-piece = *prominent thing;* The Taj is the centre-piece of Agra.

Centre-stage = *important position;* The economic policy takes centre-stage of discussion.

Change one's tune = *show different opinion;* Politicians change their tunes often.

Charisma = *charm inspiring devotion;* Abraham Lincoln had a charisma about him.

Charismatic figure = *compelling attention;* Gandhiji was a charismatic figure.

Charm offensive = *to flatter to win support;* The party is on a charm offensive against angry members.

Chartbuster = *great success;* The new album of Asha Bhonsle is a chartbuster.

Chart out = *make;* I will chart out my own career.

Chat show = *TV or Radio programme;* He has gone for a chat show.

Cheese off = *feel boredom;* I feel cheesed off with this story.

Chequered career = *of different fortunes;* Many people have chequered careers.

Cherry on the cake = *good finishing touch;* His century was the cherry on the cake.

Cherubic smile = *angelic smile;* The baby has a cherubic smile on her face.

An old chestnut = *aged and tedious;* Some players in the team are old chestnuts.

Chicken out = *get scared;* He chickened out of the fight.

Chill out = *pass time aimlessly;* Incompetent workers chill out in the office.

Chink in one's armour = *weak point;* A weak policy is a chink in an organisation's armour.

Chivvy into action = *inspire;* Good management chivvies workers into action.

Chug along = *move slowly;* Small traders are still chugging along.

City slicker = *unreliable city dwellers;* Unfortunately, some city slickers are forming wildlife policy.

Classy = *stylish, sophisticated;* It is a classy resort.

Clear-cut policy = *easy to understand;* The government should form a clear-cut policy on this issue.

A cliff hanger = *exciting, full of suspense;* The match between Brazil and Germany was a cliff hanger.

Clockwork precision = *smooth and regular;* A good organisation works with clockwork precision.

A closed chapter = *no more in existence;* We have no dealings with that firm. It is a closed chapter.

Close-run = *win or lose by a narrow margin;* It was a close-run victory. We won by two runs.

On cloud nine = *very happy;* Germany has won the World Cup, and they are on cloud nine.

A lot of clout = *power, influence;* He carries a lot of clout with the management.

Live in clover = *live in luxury;* People with high income live in clover.

Clear away the cobwebs = *remove;* Let us clear away the cobwebs of corruption.

Clear the deck = *clear ground;* The decks are clear for his inclusion in the team.

Cold comfort = *little, poor;* The incentive which the firm gave was cold comfort for the workers.

The cold shoulder = *neglect, reject;* A successful organisation gives the cold shoulder to incompetent workers.

Out in the cold = *ignore;* Rich countries leave the poor countries out in the cold.

Cold storage = *postpone;* The plan has been put in cold storage.

On a collision course = *in conflict;* The workers are on a collision course with the management.

Make a comeback = *a return;* Sometimes, old fashions make a comeback.

Cold feeling = *fear;* The idea of war sends a cold feeling down my spine.

Consumer boom = *prosperity;* There is a consumer boom in India.

Consumer budget = *which consumer can afford;* We offer goods at consumer budget.

Cook up a storm = *become very popular;* The new watch will cook up a storm in the fashion world.

Crusader's zeal = *do with passion;* One should do one's work with crusader's zeal.

Curtain has come down = *end of a thing;* The curtain has come down on Roberto Carlo's career.

Choke off = *stop;* Corruption chokes off economic growth.

Claw one's way out = *recover;* By hard work we can claw our way out of a crisis.

A chip above = *slightly above;* The weight of this product is a chip above others.

Casanova image = *flirting nature;* Some Hollywood actors have developed a Casanova image.

Have a crush on = *love affair;* Hitler had a crush on Stefina.

Clear the deck = *clear the way;* A transparent policy will clear the deck for economic growth.

Cash strapped = *short of funds;* The club is cash strapped.

Catapult to = *send higher;* Your new career will catapult you to new heights.

Winning career = *successful;* Good technical training will ensure you a winning career.

Career hoppers = *who change career;* There are many career hoppers around.

Get cosy = *get friendly;* She is getting cosy with me.

Cut the crap = *come to the point;* Let us cut the crap and know the reasons of our defeat.

Copper-bottomed guarantee = *reliable, certain;* Banks require a copper-bottomed guarantee before they sanction loan.

Round the corner = *very close;* The World Cup is round the corner.

The cornerstone = *important feature;* Economic development is the cornerstone of our policy.

Crack the whip = *use force, power;* The party cracks the whip against erring members.

Crank out = *give, produce;* A good school cranks out good results.

Cream off = *take away;* Good business houses cream off competent executives from others.

Creamy layer = *elite, high profile;* These schemes will benefit the creamy layers of society.

Give credence to = *accept as true;* I don't give credence to your story.

Come a cropper = *blank or defeated;* In the tournament, our team has come a cropper.

At cross purposes = *have different aims;* The two brothers were at cross purposes.

Cross one's mind = *occur, come;* Suddenly, the idea crossed my mind.

Crossroads = *time to take decision;* Our civilisation is at a crossroads.

Crowning glory = *the best part;* Your speech was the crowning glory of the function.

Crowning asset = *very useful thing;* Good executives are the crowning assets of a company.

Culture vulture = *person fond of arts;* He is a culture vulture.

Curtain lecture = *a wife's scolding of husband;* A wife often gives curtain lecture to her husband.

Cut out for = *fit;* You are cut out for the teaching profession.

Cut-throat competition = *tough;* This is an age of cut-throat competition.

Cutting edge = *advantageous position;* By hard work our company is at the cutting edge.

A cut above = *superior;* Sachin is a cut above the rest.

Cut-price = *sale at low price;* They are selling cut-price watches.

Computer-friendly = *fond of computer;* We are computer-friendly.

Cyberphobia = *fear of computer;* Some people have cyberphobia.

Czar = *a man with great power;* Bill Gates is a computer czar.

Time chance = *great opportunity;* Here is your time chance.

Winning career = *bright career;* We ensure you a winning career.

Get cracking = *hurry up;* You better get cracking if you want to catch the train.

Intellectual capital = *brain power;* Business houses rely on intellectual capital of executives.

From close quarters = *thoroughly;* I know him from close quarters.

D

Dab hand = *expert;* He is a dab hand at badminton.

Daft question = *foolish;* Don't ask daft questions.

Dainty appetite = *difficult and fastidious;* He has dainty appetite.

Damage-control exercise = *to control damage;* The leader is coming on a damage-control exercise.

Put a damper on = *depressing effects;* A lot of criticism put a damper on the actor's performance.

A damp squib = *an event below expectations;* Our performance at the World Cup proved a damp squib.

Dance to one's tune = *completely follow other's order;* A respected man never dances to another's tune.

Danger man = *a man posing danger;* Spin bowlers regard Dhoni as a danger man.

Keep someone dangling = *keep in suspense;* Never keep your friends dangling.

Dance macabre = *death and destruction;* The US has unleashed a dance macabre in Iraq.

Shot in the dark = *simply a guess;* What you said was only a shot in the dark.

Darling of the crowd = *a famous person;* Sachin is the darling of the crowd.

Dark horse = *a man of hidden qualities;* The Chinese sprinter beat all and proved a dark horse.

Look dashing = *attractive;* The actor looks dashing.

A daunting task = *difficult;* To win an Olympic medal is a daunting task.

Call it a day = *decide to retire;* Pete Sampras and Andre Agassi have called it a day.

Reach a dead-end = *reach the end;* The negotiations are at a dead-end.

A raw deal = *harsh treatment;* Immigrants generally receive a raw deal from the authorities.

A square deal = *fair treatment;* The management should give a square deal to good workers.

Deal a death blow = *an action which ends something;* The recent bombing dealt a death blow to peace efforts.

Debonair and dashing = *a handsome man;* He looks debonair and dashing.

Deep-dyed = *complete;* I am deep-dyed football fan.

Deep-laid plan = *secret;* Hitler made a deep-laid plan to defeat the Allied forces.

Deep-rooted conspiracy = *deeply implanted;* There is a deep-rooted conspiracy against you.

Delaying tactics = *plan to delay or defer;* Some players indulge in delaying tactics.

Without demur = *without objection;* She accepted the job without demur.

De novo = *anew, again;* Begin this project de novo.

In depth = *in complete detail;* Students should know a subject in depth.

De rigueur = *in fashion;* It is de rigueur now to dye hair.

Get one's just deserts = *to get reward or punishment;* All dictators get their just deserts.

Deserve a medal = *something heroic, praiseworthy;* You deserve a medal for scoring a century.

Daredevil deeds = *do daring deeds;* Test pilots perform daredevil deeds.

Damocles' sword = *a dreaded evil;* The fear of death hangs like Damocles' sword over all men.

Deadlock = *a state with no solution;* The talks have reached a deadlock.

Dead set = *firm, determined;* He is dead set to achieve his goal.

Dicey business = *dangerous thing;* Dictatorship is a dicey business.

The die is cast = *decision that can't be changed;* The die is cast in your favour.

Dig out = *find out fact after search;* The police dug up the facts about the murder.

Dilly-dally = *waste time aimlessly;* Now don't dilly-dally, and do your work.

Get off the dime = *take decision and initiative;* It's time you get off the dime and do work honestly.

By dint of = *perseverance;* He succeeded in life by dint of hard work.

Dirty money = *illegal money;* Some firms launder dirty money for smugglers.

At someone's disposal = *available for use;* This cycle is at my disposal.

Beyond dispute = *certain, sure;* What you stated was beyond dispute.

Keep one's distance = *stay far away;* Keep your distance from a dishonest man.

Within striking distance = *near the target;* The player was within striking distance, but could not score the goal.

Distressed area = *area of poverty;* There are many distressed areas in the world.

A diva = *admired woman;* Madhubala was a Bollywood diva.

Take a dive = *sudden fall;* Prices sometimes take a dive and again soar up.

Dizzy heights = *high point;* Ronaldo has reached dizzying heights.

Do away with = *remove;* Let us do away with terrorism.

To doctor = *to falsify;* He has doctored the accounts to hide his theft.

In the doldrums = *time of depression;* The industry is in the doldrums.

Dollar diplomacy = *money power to influence other countries;* The US uses dollar diplomacy.

Till doomsday = *forever;* I will be with you till doomsday.

Donkey's years = *since very long;* I have been your friend for donkey's years.

Doom and gloom = *a feeling of pessimism;* There was a feeling of doom and gloom during war.

At one's doorstep = *very near;* Our services are at your doorstep.

A doorway = *a gateway;* Hard work is a doorway to success.

On the dot = *on exact time;* I reached the airport on the dot at ten o' clock.

Double-cross = *deceive, betray;* Some greedy people double-cross their own country.

Double-dealing = *deceive, cheat;* He is known for double-dealing.

Double-quick = *very fast, quickly;* We returned in double-quick time.

Double-standard = *unfair rule;* I can never stand for double-standard and double speak.

Drag one's feet = *unwilling to act;* The firm has dragged its feet over this policy.

Draw a blank = *remain unsuccessful;* We took part in the competition, but drew a blank.

Dream up something = *imagine something;* They are dreaming up new ways to sell their product.

Dressing-down = *receive reprimand, scolding;* He received a dressing-down from his boss.

In the driver's seat = *in control;* He is in the driver's seat, you can't challenge him.

A driving force = *to have strong influence;* The prime minister is the driving force behind this scheme.

At the drop of a hat = *without reason;* He smiles at the drop of a hat.

Drop-off = *fall, decline;* Ever since the mall opened, our business has dropped off.

A drubbing = *beating, defeat;* England gave Australia a drubbing.

Drum something up = *get or obtain;* We are drumming up support for the communist candidatet.

Come up dry = *be unsuccessful;* All our efforts to change his habits have come dry.

Play ducks and drakes = *treat without seriousness;* Don't play ducks and drakes with me.

As dull as dishwater = *very dull;* The book is as dull as dishwater.

In the dumps = *unhappy;* You went and left me in the dumps.

The dust settles = *things calm down;* We think the dust would settle down, and the problem will be over.

A dust-up = *a fight;* We had a dust-up with our neighbour.

To one's dying day = *always;* I will never forget it to my dying day.

A dynamo = *powerful, energetic;* Indira Gandhi was a dynamo in Indian politics.

Leave in the dust = *surpass, superior;* Our product leaves others in the dust.

Drop the call = *take back, away;* The party has dropped its call for withdrawal from the government.

Do a ditto = *do the same;* You are a good bowler. Please do a ditto with your batting also.

Devil incarnate = *like the devil;* He is the devil incarnate.

Gets dated = *old;* This instrument will never get dated.

Download the idea = *pass, thrust;* Don't download this idea onto me.

Take a dig = *mock, criticise;* The minister took a dig at his opponents.

A Don Quixote = *a dreamy, unpractical man;* Don't be a Don Quixote. Always be a realist and practical.

Done up = *tired and exhausted;* I feel done up after this hard work.

Draconian law = *severe and tough law;* To stop terrorism we will have to make draconian laws.

To drive a roaring = *do brisk business;* During Diwali traders drive a roaring trade.

Eagle eye = *to keep a close watch;* The teacher kept an eagle eye on Smith.

No ear = *no liking, indifferent;* He has no ear for music.

Over head and ears = *wholly;* I am in debt over head and ears.

To have itching ears = *keen to hear news and gossip;* Tom's mother has itching ears.

To ease one of money = *cheat;* Bill eased Jack of his money.

Like as two eggs = *exactly alike;* Peter and Paul are as alike as two eggs.

Come back to earth = *return to reality;* After his early failures, Jim came back to earth.

Political earthquake = *create upheaval, commotion;* The attack on America created a political earthquake in the world.

Earth-shattering news = *shocking;* The murder of the leader was earth-shattering news.

Easier said than done = *difficult to put into practice;* To achieve economic targets is easier said than done.

Easy on the eye = *good to look at;* Aishwarya is easy on the eye.

Of easy virture = *morally corrupt;* Stella is a girl of easy virtue.

Easy-going = *relaxed;* Kim likes the easy-going life.

Easy-peasy = *very easy;* Fred asked easy-peasy questions.

Eaten up = *dominated;* The thief was eaten up with greed.

Ebbing away = *reducing;* His influence is now ebbing away.

At low ebb = *in bad, poor state;* Our economy is at a low ebb.

Ebb and flow = *rise and fall;* A politician faces many ebbs and flows in his career.

Ecocide = *destruction of natural habitat;* The industrialists are indulging in ecocide.

Eco-friendly = *useful to environment;* The government shoud make eco-friendly laws.

On edge = *nervous;* Students are on edge during examinations.

On razor's edge = *difficult time;* The world is walking on razor's edge.

Take the edge off = *reduce, lessen;* Good work takes the edge off all criticism.

Edutainment = *education and entertainment;* A computer is meant for edutainment.

To that effect = *with that result;* The board made a new policy, and informed the workers to that effect.

Egg on one's face = *look foolish;* The failure to find nuclear weapons in Iraq left Bush with egg on his face.

Egg on = *encourage;* A teacher should be positive, and should egg on his students.

Electrifying effect = *create thrill;* Your presence had an electrifying effect on the public.

In one's element = *natural environment;* He is looking happy and in his element.

An embattled man = *faced with problems;* He is an embattled chief minister.

All ends up = *completely;* Australia beat India all ends up.

Have come to an end = *finished, over;* Her career has come to an end.

Enfamilie = *with family;* Dom has gone out enfamilie.

Enfant terrible = *man with shocking ideas;* Hitler was an enfant terrible.

At the epicentre = *central point;* Terrorism is at the epicentre of global concerns.

Epoch-making = *great, significant;* Scientists are making epoch-making efforts in the field of medicine.

Other things being equal = *if other factors remain the same;* Obviously, other things being equal, we'll make profit.

In essence = *fundamentally, basically;* The policy looks tricky but in essence it is useful.

On an even keel = *balanced, normal;* Our relations are on an even keel.

In the event of = *if that happens;* In the event of a financial crisis, you can rely on a bank.

Exciting career = *attractive;* All competent executives look for an exciting career.

Take exception to = *object;* Dick took exception to Jim's remark.

Heated exchange = *hot words;* Moby had a heated exchange with Sam.

Make an exhibition of oneself = *behave foolishly;* Don't make an exhibition of yourself in school.

Even-handed = *fair and just;* Always follow a transparent and even-handed policy.

At someone's expense = *at other's cost;* You enjoy all facilities at my expense.

Close one's eyes to = *refuse to notice;* One can't shut one's eyes to eternal facts.

In the eye of the storm = *centre of controversy;* He is in the eye of a political storm.

Have an eye for = *appreciate, recognise;* Jones has an eye for beauty.

Eyeball to eyeball = *face to face;* Martha had an eyeball to eyeball confrontation with Marlyn.

Eye-catching = *appealing, attractive;* Indeed, it is an eye-catching design.

Eye-popping = *huge, great;* During Christmas they make eye-popping profit.

Eyesore = *ugly, insulting;* Poverty is an eyesore for our society.

F

Face the music = *face the bad results of an action;*   The shopkeeper caught him stealing books. Now he'll face the music.

Lose face = *a loss of respect;*   He can't come to my house. He has lost face.

On the face of it = *at first glance;*   On the face of it, this policy looks weak.

A face-saving device = *retain respect;*   This step is only a face-saving device.

Set one's face against = *oppose, resist;*   The members have set their faces against the board's policy.

To one's face = *openly;*   I can say this fact to his face.

Face-to-face = *direct;*   Jim came face-to-face with a tiger.

The fact of the matter = *reality, the truth;*   The fact of the matter is that you are incompetent.

Current fad = *a craze;*   The current fad is to make TV serials.

Fail-safe = *unable to fail;*   We want fail-safe technology.

Fair and square = *completely, honestly;*   I defeated him fair and square.

Fair-weather friend = *friend of happy times only;*   Job is a fair-weather friend.

Fair name = *good respect, reputation;*   We have a fair name in the market.

Fall in with = *agree to;*   Bob fell in with my views.

Fall through = *fail;*   The project finally fell through.

A falling-out = *a fight, quarrel;*   Tim and Tom had a falling-out.

A fall-off = *a decrease;*   There is fall-off in our profit.

Fancy-free = *not fully committed;*   Jone's wife is footloose and fancy-free.

Farmyard language = *bad, ill mannered;*   He talked to me in farmyard language.

A farrago = *a mixture;*   This book is a farrago of nonsense.

On fast lane = *a hectic lifestyle;*   In this age we live on a fast lane.

Feast one's eyes on = *look at with pleasure;*   I was feasting my eyes on the beautiful scenery.

A remarkable feat = *a great achievement;*   Computer is a remarkable feat of technology.

Feather one's nest = *make illicit money;*   A greedy man always feathers his nest.

Feel the pulse = *know;*   A good leader feels the pulse of society.

Feel-good movie = *cause happiness;*   Only few directors make feel-good movies.

Sit on the fence = *not to make any decision;*   When a tricky situation arises, the shrewd politician sits on the fence.

To ferret out = *search out;*   The police inspector has ferreted out the facts.

In fine fettle = *good condition;* The TV is in fine fettle.

To fend off = *to evade something to protect oneself;* Rock fended of all questions.

To fine-tune = *make changes to get the best result;* The professor is fine-tuning his lecture.

Finger-licking = *delicious, tasty;* It is a finger-licking preparation.

At one's fingertips = *readily available;* All facts are at my fingertips.

Catch fire = *become popular;* The film will catch fire.

Firing on all cylinders = *work at top level;* The students should fire on all cylinders to get top position.

To set the world on fire = *a very exciting thing;* This new discovery will set the world on fire.

Firebrand = *a person dedicated to a cause;* He is a Communist firebrand.

Give firepower = *make more attacking;* The new policy will give more firepower to the traders.

In the firing line = *facing criticism, blame;* The workers are in the firing line.

Fit the bill = *suitable, fit;* There is a vacancy and you will fit the bill.

By fits and starts = *irregularly;* The project is going on by fits and starts.

To fizzle out = *end or fail;* The revolution has fizzled out.

A flagship product = *the most important, the best;* This cement is the flagship product of the company.

To flame out = *fail;* He flamed out in the first round.

Flash in the pan = *brief success;*   Our early success was only a flash in the pan.

Flat out = *very fast, straightaway;*   We went flat out and defeated them.

Fatal flaw = *main defect, fault;*   Greed is the fatal flaw in his character.

Flex one's muscles = *show power, strength;*   Union workers are flexing their muscles.

The flower of = *the finest and best people;*   IIT students are the flowers of our country.

A fluke = *by chance or luck;*   Our victory was not a fluke.

Flummox and fluster = *confused and perplex;*   I feel flummoxed and flustered to hear your story.

Fly into a rage = *become angry;*   When Shane saw me he flew into a rage.

Fly-by-night = *dishonest, unreliable;*   Ray is a fly-by-night businessman.

Focal point = *centre, main point;*   Ecology is the focal point of the book.

Foible and fooly = *weaknesses;*   We see foibles and foolies of human life.

Follow one's nose = *trust oneself;*   A right person follows his nose.

To do footwork = *correct and sensible changes;*   Business houses have to do a lot of footwork in the face of competition.

To the fore = *come on top;*   The question of taxes came to the fore during discussion.

Forget-me-not = *not be forgotten;*   She looked at me with a forget-me-not smile.

On-form = *performing well;* We should select on-form players for the team.

Forty winks = *short sleep during the day;* The old man enjoys forty winks.

Foul one's nest = *damage one's own interest;* A wise man never fouls his own nest.

Foul mouth = *use bad language;* Cook has a foul mouth.

Founding father = *a man who starts a movement;* Lincoln was the founding father of democracy.

Four-square = *firm, strong and resolute;* Gandhiji was a four-square leader of our nation.

To fox = *deceive;* Tom can never fox me.

Foxy = *deceitful, cunning;* She is very foxy.

Fraught with = *full of danger;* The new policy is fraught with danger.

Fitness freak = *very keen about health;* The boys are fitness freaks.

Free-for-all = *a fight;* Then a free-for-all started.

Freeloader = *living on other's generosity;* Jill does no work. She is a freeloader.

Freeze one's blood = *fill with fear;* The story of the maneater freezes my blood.

Full of beans = *happy, in high spirit;* Dean is full of beans.

Funereal silence = *complete;* There was funereal silence in the valley.

On the forefront = *on top, be a leader;* We are on the forefront of technology.

Go full throttle = *with full steam;* France went full throttle against Brazil.

Back in the fray = *make a comeback;* The South African team is back in the fray.

Fresh lease of life = *give new energy, dimension;* The new policy will give a fresh lease of life to the industrial sector.

Fire the first salvo = *aggressive act, criticism;* He fired the first salvo against the minister.

Take one's foot off the accelerator = *get slow and slack;* The team took its foot off the accelerator and lost the match.

Fire up = *start, begin;* The entry of MNCs has fired up a revolution in India.

On the fret = *angry, sulky;* He is always on the fret.

Family and fortune = *of good family and rich;* Sarah is a girl of family and fortune.

Between two fires = *facing two problems;* The Republican party is between two fires.

On firm footing = *on strong ground;* Our business is on firm footing.

Fix the problem = *solve;* We should fix our problems.

In full flow = *top form;* Ponting is in full flow.

G

Gain on = *come close, near;* The tiger is gaining on the deer.

Gainsay = *contradict, deny;* This statement can't be gainsaid.

Play to the gallery = *act to appeal to public;* The politicians generally play to the gallery.

Game plan = *a plan made in advance;* Every party makes a game plan for its success.

Gang up = *join together;* The boys ganged up on Tom and took away his money.

Gargantuan status = *very high;* He has a gargantuan status in society.

Run out of gas = *lack power, energy;* The marathon runner is running out of gas.

Gatecrash = *enter without ticket;* The opportunist people gatecrash into the leading party.

A gateway = *a means to achieve success;* Only hardwork is a sure gateway to success.

Gear for = *prepared, ready;* That country is gearing for war.

Gear up = *preparing oneself;* The hotels are gearing up to meet the tourist influx.

Germane to = *related to;* What you say is not germane to our policy.

Get ahead = *to become successful;* I know how to get ahead in journalism.

Giant-killer = *defeat more powerful opponent;* Our ordinary team proved a giant-killer in the tournament.

Gala day = *a festive day;* We had a gala day yesterday.

A galaxy = *impressive people or things;* We have a galaxy of talent in India.

Gall and wormwood = *worthless;* Pete is gall and wormwood to his family.

Make a game = *mock, annoy;* You are making a game of me.

In good gear = *in good condition;* My computer is in good gear.

Out of gear = *not in working condition;* The TV set is out of gear.

Get by heart = *memorise;* Get this poem by heart.

Gird up one's loins = *prepare oneself;* Examinations are at hand;so gird up your loins.

Glean information = *gather, collect;* Colins gleans information from books.

Glimmer of hope = *slight, faint;* There is a glimmer of hope for his survival.

Glitterati = *elite and fashionable people;* The glitterati were present on her wedding.

Gloves are off = *something brutal to happen;*   Gloves are off and the two countries are ready to fight.

From the word go = *from the beginning;*   Bill began to hit hard from the word go.

Go great guns = *proceed with force;*   Presently, the company is going great guns.

Have a go at = *attack, criticise;*   Sophia always has a go at her neighbour.

Go around with = *move in the company of;*   Sheila goes around with a boy.

Go in for = *enter a competition;*   I am going in for an interview.

Go for = *select, choose;*   I will go for this watch.

Go-ahead = *order, permission;*   The authorities have given the go-ahead for this new branch.

Going concern = *profit-making business;*   Our's is a going concern.

Golden boy = *famous and successful;*   Sachin is the golden boy of Indian cricket.

Goof = *mistake;*   He goofed up.

Goofy = *foolish;*   She is goofy.

Make the grade = *succeed, reach desired aim;*   Hardworking students make the grade in examinations.

Grandstand view = *complete;*   The hotel gives you a grandstand view of the mountains.

Hear on the grapevine = *through rumour;*   I heard on the grapevine that he is coming.

Graphic account = *vivid and in detail;* He gave a graphic account of the war.

Grapple with = *face a problem, challenge;* The city is grappling with the problem of water shortage.

Grassroots level = *at the basic level;* We should prepare players at grassroots level.

Quiet as the grave = *very quiet;* He was as quiet as the grave.

Gravy train = *make money with little efforts;* Go to America and get on to the gravy train.

Grey areas = *not properly defined situations;* There are many grey areas in our policies.

To grill = *ask questions;* The minister was grilled in Parliament.

Come to grips with = *deal or understand;* You will have to come to grips with this problem.

Gasp for breath = *require immediate help;* The plan gasps for breath.

Break new ground = *do something new;* India is breaking new ground in technology.

Gain ground = *become popular;* This idea is fast gaining ground.

Hold one's ground = *not to retreat;* Our forces are holding their ground.

Good grounding = *basic training;* Students require good grounding in science.

Ground rules = *basic principles;* A businessman should know the ground rules of trade.

Money-grubber = *amass money;*   He is a money-grubber.

Bear a grudge = *have a feeling of ill will;*   We bear no grudge against you.

Off guard = *catch by surprise;*   The police caught the robber off guard.

Big gun = *important man;*   The minister is a big gun.

Jump the gun = *act before proper time;*   The sprinter jumped the gun and was disqualified.

Gut issue = *important part;*   The gut issue of our life is that we should be honest.

Man of guts = *brave, courageous;*   Jim Corbett was a man of guts.

A glamour girl = *attractive, fashionable;*   During beauty contest one can see many glamour girls.

Gutter children = *of low birth;*   In poor countries there are a number of gutter children.

Gutter culture = *low and indecent;*   He is a man of gutter culture.

Gain currency = *attractive, appealing;*   New technology is gaining currency in the market.

Guessing game = *simply a guess, uncertain;*   The guessing game is over.

Gun for = *act against;*   The government guns for spurious drugs.

All guns blazing = *with triumph;*   The victorious team has returned with all guns blazing.

Hyper growth = *robust, above normal;*   A good company believes in hyper growth.

Gung-ho = *keen, excited;* We are gung-ho about the future.

Umbrella group = *branches;* There are some umbrella groups of Al Qaida.

Gain ground = *become acceptable;* New ideas are gaining ground in society.

Lay the groundwork = *prepare the base;* We lay the groundwork for implementing the scheme.

A groundswell of something = *opinion of large number of people;* There is a groundswell of public anger.

Go slam-bang = *with force, power;* He went slam-bang and silenced his critics.

A gem = *a fantastic thing;* It is a gem of a book.

Get the axe = *dismiss, terminate;* His work was not satisfactory and he got the axe.

Perpetual grindstone = *a permanent trouble;* Rita acts upon me as a perpetual grindstone.

Give a go = *start, begin;* Now we should give a go to this policy.

Settle into a groove = *take up a position;* When the coach settled into a groove, the captain dropped a bombshell.

Give arms to = *give force, power;* We should give arms to the policy.

In general air = *in fashion, common;* To keep long hair is in general air.

Gee-whiz technology = *wonderful;* This is an era of gee-whiz technology.

Go to the green pastures = *go to a place to make money;* Computer engineers are going to green pastures.

Have the gumption = *courage, initiative;* He has the gumption to start this project.

Have ghettoed mentality = *narrow;* They are slum-dwellers. They have ghettoed mentality.

Keep your gunpowder dry = *keep ready for attack;* The enemy is near. Keep your gunpowder dry.

Do one's homework well = *well-prepared;* A coach should do his homework well before the selection of the team.

Drive one's guilt away = *free from guilt;* Laker wanted to drive his guilt away.

Guard one's flank = *save oneself from attack;* I can guard my flank.

Give a big jolt = *give shock;* This news gave him a big jolt.

A greenhorn = *an inexperienced person;* Bret is a greenhorn.

Grill someone = *interrogate, question;* The judge grilled him to know the truth.

Go into a flap = *get nervous, panic;* When Hogg saw it, he went into a flap.

A go-getter = *man of courage and ambitions;* Brian is a go-getter and will succeed.

On a grandiose scale = *lavishly;* The function was arranged on a grandiose scale.

Get to the point = *waste no time;* Don't talk nonsense but get to the point.

To go by = *follow;* Always go by the rules.

Have a good rapport = *good relation;* Sheila has a good rapport with her boss.

Go off track = *remain unfocussed;* He went off track and failed.

Go over one's head = *not understandable;* What he speaks goes over my head.

A grinding task = *tedious, difficult;* It is a grinding task.

Ground reality = *basic reality;* He knows the ground reality of the situation.

Get off the ground = *begin, start, happen;* The agreement is getting off the ground.

Grow on the tree = *easily available;* Money does not grow on the tree.

Gruelling work schedule = *tiring;* Teachers have gruelling work schedules.

Grind to a halt = *stop slowly;* The work came to a grinding halt.

Grey area = *undefined situation;* There are grey areas in the plan.

Grease the palm = *bribe a person;* You grease his palm and he will do the job.

Give a graphic account = *give in detail;* He gave a graphic account of his works.

Glory day = *happy day of the past;* I recollect the glory days of my life.

Pay glowing tribute = *praise highly;* He paid glowing tribute to the leader

Grapple with a problem = *struggle, wrestle;* They are grappling with this problem.

Gala event = *entertaining social event;* I attended a gala event last night.

Galloping = *uncontrollable;* Property prices are galloping.

Galvanic effect = *dramatic, sudden;* These steps will have galvanic effects on our society.

Get to the bottom = *know the reality;* I should get to the bottom of the issue.

Galvanise the masses = *energise, activate;* His speech galvanised the masses.

A gambit = *device, ploy;* His dismissal was a gambit to win public support.

The game is up = *the deception is revealed;* You can no longer cheat us. The game is up.

Run the gamut = *to cover the complete range;* Corruption runs the entire gamut of human society.

Gang together = *form a group;* Small traders have ganged together to beat multinational companies.

In the garb of = *in the dress;* He is a devil in the garb of a friend.

Garner support = *get, gather;* Berty is garnering support for the election

Gassy = *talkative, verbose;* Cook is very gassy.

Gain momentum = *gain force;* The plan is now gaining momentum.

Gazillion of something = *large quantity;* Cliff has gazillions of caps.

Move up a gear = *put more power in a work;* West Indies team is moving up a gear.

Gear down = *bring to lower level;* You look tired. You should gear down your work.

Generate euphoria = *create great excitement;* The new book will generate euphoria in public.

Generous with = *kind, helpful;* Ron is very generous with me.

Genesis of something = *root cause, origin;* Poverty is the genesis of all evils.

The gentry = *people of good position;* The costly cars are for the gentry.

Geographical barriers = *limits, boundaries;* True love conquers geographical barriers.

Genuflect to = *show respect, servility;* The traders are genuflecting to the government to get concessions.

Get ahead = *become successful;* A hardworking man gets ahead in his career.

Get along with = *move and live with;* Bob can get along with Linda.

Get away = *escape;* The dacoit got away easily.

Get back to = *be in touch with;* The boss will get back to you soon.

Get in with = *come in contact;* Children should not get in with bad people.

Get out = *become known;* If this information gets out, we will be in trouble.

Get over = *recover from sad experience;* You pray to God and you will get over your sorrow.

Get round = *accept;* In due course you will get round to my views.

Get through = *pass, succeed;* Lin got through the examination.

Ghost of a chance = *no chance;*   I don't stand the ghost of a chance to get this job.

Ghostly appearance = *like a ghost;*   The old man has a ghostly appearance.

Glided youth = *young wealthy people;*   Paul moves with the glided youth of the town.

A gimmick = *device to get attention;*   This show is a gimmick to get votes.

Give air = *speak with pride;*   Peter always gives air to himself.

Give and take = *on mutual basis;*   We businessmen believe in give and take policy.

Not give a damn = *don't care at all;*   We generally don't give a damn about the poor.

Give someone away = *reveal, show;*   Your bad deeds will give you away one day.

Give in = *yield, surrender;*   The murderer gave in to intense questioning.

Give out = *exhausted, finished;*   All my money is giving out.

Glam girl = *beautiful, attractive;*   Clara is a glam girl.

At first glance = *when seen for the first time;*   I fell in love with her at first glance.

Glance through = *read quickly;*   The girl is glancing through the pages.

Catch a glimpse = *see briefly;*   I caught a glimpse of the queen.

Glittering career = *bright;*   Rodny has a glittering career in this organisation.

Go-getter = *enterprising man;*   Wishy is a go-getter and will succeed.

A gold mine = *source of valuable thing;*   Rick is a gold mine of knowledge.

Be in good grace = *regard with favour;*   He is in good grace of the principal.

Gravity of the situation = *seriousness;*   They are careful and know the gravity of the situation.

Great divide = *difficult distinction;*   There is a great divide between the rich and the poor.

Give the green light = *permission;*   The management has given the green light to the workers to finish the project.

One's guts out = *do with determination;*   Ben worked his guts out and succeeded.

Gubernatorial status = *very big;*   Abe always tries to get a gubernatorial status.

Generic cause = *not specific;*   There may be some generic cause of mental illness.

Within hall = *within calling distance;*   Neil is within hall.

A hair's breath = *narrowly;*   The soldier escaped death by a hair's breath.

Hair-splitting = *find small fault;*   She has hair-splitting nature.

Hair-trigger = *violent temperament;*   He has a hair-trigger temperament.

Halcyon days = *happy days of the past;*   We remember the halcyon days of our youth.

Half measures = *incomplete, not enough;*   A good organisation never believes in half measures.

A hallmark = *especial feature;*   Durability is a hall mark of our product.

Call a halt = *stop;*   We called a halt to any further talk.

Hammer out = *work out;*   The government is hammering out a solution of the problem.

Be hamstrung = *restricted;*   The project was hamstrung by lack of resources.

At hand = *near, close by;*   The examinations are at hand.

Hands down = *easily;*   Don won the match hands down.

Hands off = *not to touch, control;* Keep your hands off this project.

On hand = *need to be done;* We have many works on hand.

Handshaking distance = *very near;* The tiger was within handshaking distance.

Come in handy = *prove useful;* One day this book will come in handy.

Get the hang of = *learn to do;* The computer is simple to operate when you get the hang of it.

Hang around = *loiter, move aimlessly;* The boys hang around the school.

Hanger-on = *man with personal interest;* There are many hangers-on in politics.

Hanker after = *desire to get;* He hankers after a cosy job.

Hard-boiled = *realistic and tough;* He is a hard-boiled reporter.

Make a hash = *spoil, bungle;* The player made a hash of this golden chance.

Hassle-free = *without trouble;* The tourists require hassle-free journey.

Hawk-eyed = *careful, vigilant;* Sam is a hawk-eyed teacher.

Go haywire = *go out of control;* The plan has gone haywire.

Come to a head = *reach a critical point;* Disorder and chaos came to a head with the arrest of the leader.

Get something into head = *understand;* Get this important idea into your head.

Heads will roll = *workers will be dismissed;* If we implement this policy, many heads will roll.

A head start = *advantageous position;* A good training will give you a head start.

Off one's head = *crazy;* Tim is off his head these days.

Put heads together = *work together;* Let us put our heads together to find out a solution.

To headbutt = *hit with head;* Zidane headbutted an Italian defender.

Hats off to = *to honour or praise;* Hats off to Jim Corbett for killing maneaters all alone.

Headlong = *with head foremost;* There was a headlong collision between two buses.

At heart = *one's real nature;* My mother is good at heart.

Break heart = *make sad;* The news of his death broke my heart.

Put heart in = *work sincerely;* Put your heart in your work.

Heart-stopping = *thrilling, very exciting;* Sophia told me a heart-stoppping story.

Take the heat out = *take away the pressure;* The authorities took the heat out of argument.

Heart-to-heart = *frank, open;* They had a heart-to-heart conversation.

In seventh heaven = *very happy;* When the girl got the prize, she was in seventh heaven.

Heavyweight = *person of importance;* He is an economic heavyweight.

On his heels = *coming closely after;*   The police is on the heels of a robber.

Take to new heights = *at top place;*   This career will take you to new heights.

All hell broke loose = *disorder, chaos;*   When the monkey entered the class, all hell broke loose.

Here and now = *at the very present moment;*   I will finish my work here and now.

Hereabouts = *close to this place;*   There is a dense forest hereabouts.

Het up = *feel angry, agitated;*   Jill is het up about my behaviour.

Face hiccups = *difficulty, setback;*   Everybody faces some hiccups in life.

Give a hiding = *beating;*   Dane's father gave him a hiding.

High and dry = *in difficulty;*   They are feeling high and dry after being dismissed from their job.

The high ground = *superior position;*   Our party is on the moral high ground.

On high horse = *pompous behaviour;*   Dorris is always on her high horse.

High gear = *in top position;*   The team is in high gear.

High jinks = *happy mood;*   Ron is in high jinks.

High-water mark = *at maximum level;*   Terrorism is at a high-water mark.

Highway and byway = *main and minor roads;*   I have passed through highways and byways of life.

To the hilt = *completely;*   We will support you to the hilt.

Take a hint = *understand;* She took the hint and ran away.

Hire and fire = *employ for short time;* The management believes in a hire and fire policy.

Go down in history = *recorded in history;* Gandhiji's name has gone down in history.

Make history = *to be remembered in history;* Our victory at the World Cup made history.

Hit-or-miss = *not certain, only a possibility;* Your work can be hit-or-miss.

Make a hit = *become popular;* This song made a big hit.

A hive of activity = *a place of great activity;* The Parliament is a hive of activity.

Go the whole hog = *do thoroughly;* He went the whole hog and achieved his aim.

Hold good = *remain valid;* The principle of non-violence still holds good.

Hold the line = *remain firm;* A good policy will always hold the line.

Hold water = *sound, valid;* This statement holds water.

Hold on to = *keep;* A school should hold on to experienced staff.

Hold out = *give, offer;* The new policy holds out hope for new industrialists.

Make a hole = *take away, ruin;* It will make a big hole in our profits.

Hone up = *sharpen, make more efficient;* Practice will hone up your skill.

Off the hook = *set free, out of trouble;* You got the culprit off the hook.

Fashion heartthrob = *very fashionable;* Liza, a fashion heartthrob, is coming to our show.

Hype and hoopla = *unnecessary fuss and publicity;* Despite the hype and hoopla the firm failed.

On the hop = *busy;* The manager is on the hop.

From the horse's mouth = *reliable information;* I got it from the horse's mouth.

Hot and heavy = *intense, difficult;* The interview was hot and heavy.

Hot seat = *responsible position;* The principal is in the hot seat.

Hot stuff = *outstanding, very good;* The film is hot stuff.

House of cards = *delicately balanced;* The scheme seems like a house of cards.

Go into a huddle = *to speak about secret matters;* All party leaders have gone into a huddle.

Huff and puff = *pant, breathe heavily;* He saw a tiger and ran huffing and puffing.

Hoax and humbug = *nonsense;* This is all hoax and humbug.

Hype and headline = *intensive publicity;* Some politicians rely on hype and headlines.

Hound out = *remove forcibly;* They are hounding out Indians from their country.

In the hindsight = *to understand late;* In the hindsight we think we should have gone.

A hot potato = *a problem;*   He is a hot potato on our hands.

Hold fort = *defend;*   The goalkeeper is holding fort for Germany.

Bear hug = *tight embrace, welcome;*   When the leader came, we gave him a bear hug.

Hunky-dory = *fine;*   Everything is hunky-dory.

Over-hyped = *get extra publicity;*   Some cricketers are over-hyped media darlings.

A hotbed = *centre;*   Paris is the hotbed of fashion.

Hit the market = *appear;*   The new medicine will hit the market soon.

Heavy dose = *extra, large quantity;*   Phil received a heavy dose of criticism.

Throbbing heart = *centre of activity;*   Japan is a throbbing heart of capitalism.

Hearty and hilarious = *happy, lively;*   She is hearty and hilarious.

Strike at heart = *affect deeply;*   The economic ban will strike at the heart of industries.

Feel the heat = *feel uncomfortable;*   As the prices are going up, the government is feeling the heat.

High-voltage = *exciting, thrilling;*   It is really a high-voltage match.

Hinge on = *depend;*   A country's economy hinges on sound policy.

Head into = *enter, start;*   As we head into a business, we face many problems.

Hook to = *attach, absorbed;* Children are hooked to cyber cafes.

Make one's heart bloom = *make happy;* The beautiful valley will make your heart bloom.

Give a heady feeling = *strong effect;* The book gives a heady feeling to readers.

Heart-pounding action = *thrilling;* The movie is full of heart-pounding action.

Play havoc = *cause great damage;* The flood played havoc with our life.

Keep your hair on = *not to lose temper;* Keep your hair on in times of trouble.

Hard and fast = *fixed, certain;* There are no hard and fast rules.

Hard feelings = *ill feeling;* Ron has no hard feelings against you.

Hard-headed person = *a realist;* Businessmen are generally hard-headed.

A harum-scarum person = *reckless;* She is a harum-scarum girl.

Have a dekko = *see, look at;* Have a dekko at the picture.

Hatch up something = *devise, make;* They hatched up a plan.

Make headway = *progress;* All our efforts made little headway.

Heart-breaking news = *cause distress;* His death was heart-breaking news.

Heart-to-heart talk = *close, intimate;*   I will have heart-to-heart talk with you.

Something heating up = *get intense, excited;*   The match is heating up.

Heavy going = *difficult situation;*   We found the talk heavy going.

Something heavyweight = *important, significant;*   He is a political heavyweight.

Take to heels = *escape, run away;*   He saw the police and took to his heels.

At the height of = *at the top;*   I am at the height of my career.

Take to new heights = *to greater fame;*   They are taking tehnology to new heights.

Hell-bent = *bent upon to get;*   Jill is hell-bent to start her own business.

A high-flyer = *a person of potential;*   Simpson is a high-flyer.

Highjack something = *take forcibly;*   Ross highjacked my plan.

Get to the heart of the problem = *know the truth;*   You should get to the heart of the problem before you take any action.

To hit the ceiling = *very high;*   The prices are hitting the ceiling.

Ho-hum = *a work of poor quality;*   What you do is ho-hum.

Go in a huff = *leave with anger;*   He left the room in a huff.

High words = *angry words;*   Both the boys exchanged high words.

Become hip = *a fashion;* It is becoming hip to visit the cybercafe.

A howler = *a stupid mistake;* The article was a howler.

Out of habit = *because of;* Neil and Viola read together out of habit.

Old hag = *ugly old woman;* Martha is an old hag.

Handful of = *small number;* Only a handful of people were present.

Handsome tribute = *rich compliments;* He paid handsome tribute to the president.

Hard hit = *badly affected;* The area was hard hit by cyclone.

Run with the hare & hunt with hounds = *good with both parties;* He runs with the hare and hunts with hounds.

Come to no harm = *remain undamaged;* There was violence all around but I came to no harm.

Hawkish policy = *aggressive;* They follow a hawkish policy.

Heading for = *moving;* You are heading for trouble.

A headspring = *main source;* A mother is a headspring of real joy for children.

Have a heart of gold = *kind, generous;* Allworthy had a heart of gold.

Turn the heat = *put pressure;* The bowler is turning the heat on the batsman.

In the heat of the moment = *temporary anger;* Gill used these words in the heat of the moment.

Ham-handed approach = *half-hearted;* You can't succeed with this ham-handed approach.

Hammer and tongs = *with energy, interest;* He is working hammer and tongs.

A big hand = *great applause;* He has won the race. Give him a big hand.

Happy-go-lucky = *cheerful;* Rita is a happy-go-lucky girl.

Hark back = *remember from past;* Don't hark back on your past achievements.

Harrowing time = *difficult;* I had a harrowing time with him.

Grab the headline = *important item, prominence;* The man-eater of Rudraprayag once grabbed the headlines.

Keep one's head = *remain quiet, calm;* Keep your head in times of trouble.

Turn head = *attract attention;* These obscene pictures turned heads.

Heads-up = *warning;* We received the heads-up about the cyclone.

Hearts and mind = *intellectual support;* They are trying to win hearts and mind of the public.

Take to heart = *take seriously;* He took to heart what I said to him.

Heart-warming = *profitable, useful;* I had a heart-warming discussion with my friend.

Hefty amount = *large;* This is a hefty amount.

Get the hell out of = *escape, leave;* We should get the hell out of this bad place.

Play hell = *destroy, damage;* The children played hell with my books.

Something hellish = *very unpleasant;* It is a hellish time for all of us.

A helping hand = *give assistance;* Please give a helping hand to this poor girl.

A Herculean task = *difficult, tough;* To finish this job in one day is a Herculean task.

High spot = *the most important part;* A visit to the pyramids was the high spot of our tour.

A high-test product = *of high standard;* It is a high-test product and you may purchase it.

Live high on the hog = *luxurious life;* People of European countries live high on the hog.

In the hole = *in debt;* The poor farmer is in the hole.

Drive something home = *make something understood;* During discussion I drive home my point.

Hit home = *achieve the aim;* Jack's argument hit home.

Hone up something = *sharpen;* A writer hones up his literary implements.

Horse sense = *common sense;* The diplomat is lacking horse sense.

Break the ice = *release pressure, tension;* The talks reached a deadlock, but the secretary broke the ice and discussions began anew.

On thin ice = *in delicate position;* Ricky is skating on thin ice.

The tip of the iceberg = *a small part of the problem;* The bribe he took was only the tip of the iceberg.

Ice-cold = *very cold;* He drinks ice-cold water.

The icing on the cake = *extra attractive addition;* Your farewell speech was the icing on the cake.

An icon = *venerated, respected figure;* Charlton Heston was a Hollywood icon.

Have no idea = *know nothing;* I have no idea where I have kept the book.

Put ideas into head = *suggest new thoughts;* I have put these ideas into Tom's head.

Identity crisis = *a time of uncertainty;* The minister is facing an identity crisis.

Idiot box = *a TV set;* They watch serials on their idiot box.

If I were you = *a piece of advice;* If I were you, I would have accepted the job.

Ignoramus = *a foolish man;* Paul is an ignoramus.

Ill at ease = *uncomfortable;* He is feeling ill at ease.

Ill-bred = *rude, rough;* They are ill-bred children.

Ill-fated = *unluckly, doomed to fail;* Mallory and Irving went on an ill-fated expedition.

Ill-founded = *baseless, unreliable;* These concepts are ill-founded.

Under the illusion = *mistaken belief;* Dora was under the illusion that her house was haunted.

Fire with imagination = *fill with new ideas;* The poets are fired with imagination.

Man of improbity = *dishonest, wicked;* He is a man of improbity.

Be in for = *face unpleasant thing;* They are in for some trouble.

In with = *familiar, friendly;* Garry is in with many businessmen.

The ins and outs = *know in details;* Dicky Bird knows the ins and outs of cricket.

By inches = *narrowly;* The bullet missed him by inches.

Every inch = *completely;* You are every inch a nobleman.

Inch by inch = *slowly;* We covered the forest inch by inch.

On the increase = *go up;* The prices are on the increase.

Indian Summer = *happy period late in life;* The old man is enjoying an Indian Summer.

Infotainment = *entertain and information;* TV is meant for infotainment.

On one's own initiative = *by oneself;* I went there on my own initiative.

Take the initiative = *first to take action;* He took initiative and settled the problem.

Had a good innings = *good time and career;* Miller had a good innings in the advertising industry.

Know inside out = *know thoroughly;* Peter knows Paul inside out.

Instead of = *in place of;* They go by train instead of going by bus.

To all intents and purposes = *from all respects;* The boy, to all intents and purposes, is very bright.

With intent = *with the intention;* I help you with intent to make you successful.

In the interest = *for the profit;* Cut down the profit in the interest of poor consumers.

Of interest = *very interesting;* The book is of great interest.

At intervals = *not continuously;* He works at intervals.

Inward-looking = *uninterested in others;* Julie is an inward-looking girl.

Iron hand = *with ruthlessness;* Hitler ruled with an iron hand.

Iron out = *remove;* She ironed out differences between the members.

Ironclad guarantee = *solid, strong;* Give me an ironclad guarantee that you'll return the money.

At issue = *Something under discussion;* Cross-border terrorism is at issue between two countries.

Make an issue of = *treat as a problem;* Children make an issue of small things.

At it = *do, perform;* He is at his old tricks.

An itching palm = *greedy;* Sarah has an itching palm.

Ivory tower = *away from reality;* Jane Austen looked at the world from an ivory tower.

In terms of = *regarding;* Ted is doing well in terms of business.

In face of = *in front of;* He keeps his cool in face of dangers.

In view of = *because of;* Make new laws in view of new situations.

Ignite debate = *spark, create;* Terrorism has ignited a debate all over the world.

Reach an impasse = *disagreement;* Talks between the two countries have reached an impasse.

In style = *beautifully;* They finish their work in style.

In a dilemma = *undecided, confused;* I don't know what to do. I am in a dilemma.

Give an indepth insight = *complete view;* Give an indepth insight into the entire system.

Ink the deal = *sign an agreement;* The company inked the deal worth Rs.200 crores.

In line with = *in harmony;* It is not in line with modern style.

In the thick of = *deeply involved;* Kallis is in the thick of controversy.

In absentia = *when not present;* Justin and Jason will be tried in absentia.

Leave imprint on = *leave marks;* The picture left imprints on my mind.

Imbued with = *inspired with;* Her life was imbued with love and mercy.

In the image of = *closely resembling;* Mac is in the image of his father.

Of one's ilk = *similar to, like;* All doctors of John's ilk are competent.

Have an inkling = *little knowledge;* Denis gave me an inkling of his nature.

No iota of doubt = *not at all;* There is no iota of doubt about his honesty.

In deep water = *in great trouble;* His family is in deep water.

In double quick time = *very soon;* He will return in double quick time.

In context = *in present situation;* Your statement is irrelevant in the present context.

In view of = *because of;* Bobby got light punishment in view of his poor health.

Hedge the issue = *avoid;* Gill is trying to hedge the issue.

In harmony = *peace, agreement;* I am in harmony with you.

In good time = *not late;* Andrew reached the station in good time.

In good faith = *honestly;* Neil told me about the girl in good faith.

In tow = *accompanying;* Daisy went to the party with two children in tow.

In the teeth of = *despite the furious opposition;* We defended the goal in the teeth of furious attack.

In a shambles = *in chaos, disorder;* The market is in a shambles after the bomb blast.

In good shape = *good condition;* The book is in good shape.

In one's senses = *fully aware;* I know what you said. I was in my senses.

In the making = *in the process of development;* The project is in the making.

In tandem = *one after another;* Steps are being taken in tandem.

Ignite upheaval = *arouse strongly;* Your statement will ignite upheaval in society.

Ill-gotten gains = *get by unfair means;* He is making ill-gotten gains.

In an imbroglio = *confused situation;* As the examinations have been cancelled, the students find themselves in an imbroglio.

An incisive remark = *focussed, pointed;* Titus made an incisive remark on the policy.

Operate incognito = *move without true identity;* The terrorists are operating incognito.

Infra dig = *take as an insult;* Harris took my remark as an infra dig.

In toto = *completely;* I agree with you in toto.

Irruption of revolution = *forceful entry;* There was an irruption of social revolution in Russia.

J

I'm all right, Jack = *expressing self complacency;* You need not worry. I'm all right, Jack.

On one's jack = *self-dependent;* Tim requires no help. He is on his own jack.

Jack up = *hike up, increase;* The traders jacked up the prices.

Jack-in-office = *ordinary self important man;* Frank is only a jack-in-office.

Hit the jackpot = *unexpected success;* The show hit the jackpot.

Jam on the top = *a pleasant thing;* He wants a cosy and comfortable job and with jam on the top.

Jam-packed = *crowded;* The room was jam-packed with children.

Jaws of death = *a narrow escape;* The doctors saved me from the jaws of death.

The jeering crowd = *rude and mocking;* He was surrounded by the jeering crowd.

Jeremiad = *woeful tale;* The poor man told me his jeremiad.

In jest = *as a joke;* Phil said it in jest.

Jet black hair = *glossy black;*   She has jet black hair.

Jet-set = *wealthy, cosy;*   People of modern age like the jet-set lifestyle.

Jettison the plan = *give up, drop;*   Now jettison the plan for public benefit.

The jewel in the crown = *valuable thing, person;*   Tagore was a jewel in the crown of India.

Jibe at = *mock, insult;*   He jibed at his opponents.

Jigsaw puzzle = *problem;*   Drug trafficking is a jigsaw puzzle for the police.

Jinxed = *a thing that brings bad luck;*   The journey was jinxed from the very beginning.

Do the job = *achieve results;*   This paper will do the job.

On the job = *working;*   Kim is on the job.

Job's comforter = *create more distress;*   These people are only Job's comforter for the poor man.

Join battle = *start fighting;*   The two groups soon joined battle.

Join forces = *make combined efforts;*   All countries should join forces against terrorism.

Out of joint = *in disorder;*   The time is out of joint.

Get beyond a joke = *something worrying;*   The heat is getting beyond a joke.

Make a joke of = *laugh at something;*   Children are making a joke of Ken.

Full of the joys of spring = *happy and cheerful;*   The girls at the party were full of the joys of spring.

Against one's better judgement = *do insensible thing;* Oh! I did it against my better judgement.

Pass judgement = *give decision;* Please pass judgement on this issue.

Juggernaut = *a powerful force;* We can't stop the juggernaut of inflation.

Jumble sale = *sale of second-hand things;* There is a jumble sale in the market.

Jump for joy = *very happy;* When Karl got the job, he was jumping for joy.

Jump to conclusion = *form opinion in haste;* Always think and never jump to the conclusion.

One jump ahead = *ahead of others;* US athletes were one jump ahead of the Chinese.

Jump at = *accept, grab;* I will always jump at an opportunity.

Jump out = *make strong impact;* A beautiful picture will jump out at you.

Jumped-up = *undeserving person;* He is a jumped-up editor.

Jumping-off point = *starting point;* That job was the jumping-off point of my career.

The law of the jungle = *disorder, chaos;* The law of the jungle prevails in our society.

Juvenile status = *low;* Kip has a juvenile status in society.

Just on = *exactly, having just reached;* It is just on six o' clock.

A jaundiced eye = *look with prejudice;* He looks at me with a jaundiced eye.

Hold your jaw = *hold your tongue;* Now don't talk and hold your jaw.

In a jiffy = *In a minute, soon;* I will come back in a jiffy.

John Bull = *an Englishman;* He is a John Bull.

Jump at an offer = *accept eagerly;* If he gives me that cosy job,I will jump at the offer.

Jerk someone around = *deceive, cheat;* Edna jerks her employer around.

To Jolly up = *make lively, cheerful;* Roda jollied up the function.

A Judas = *unfaithful person;* Never trust Garry. He is a Judas.

Sit in judgement = *to judge other people;* You have no right to comment, because you don't sit in judgement.

Something junky = *useless;* I never read this junky stuff.

Just in case = *as a precaution;* You take this money just in case you fall short of money.

Rough justice = *unfair treatment;* Though Fred was innocent, he was given rough justice.

Within the jurisdiction = *within power;* The case is within the jurisdiction of the court.

Job definition = *qualification;* This is the job definition of the coach.

Under the jackboot = *authority;* India was under the jackboot of British rule.

Jerkwater place = *small rural place;* I often go to jerkwater places for peace.

K

Kangaroo court = *an unofficial court;* In backward countries people are tried in kangaroo courts.

Keep one's feet = *remain firm;* One should keep one's feet on the ground.

Keep open house = *provide hospitality;* Jame's mother keeps an open house.

Keep to oneself = *remain detached;* Kitty is a shy girl. She keeps to herself.

Keep something to oneself = *keep as a secret;* Please keep this story to yourself.

Keep at = *persist with;* It was a tough job but I kept at it.

Keep away = *remain away;* Always keep away from bad company.

Keep down = *keep at low level;* Keep down the population.

Keep off = *avoid;* Always keep off smoking.

Keep something off = *prevent from encroaching;* Please keep your hands off our family matter.

Keep to = *follow, stick to;* Keep to the path of truth.

Keep up with = *remain in contact;* Jane keeps up with good friends.

In someone's keeping = *under someone's care;*   Parents leave children in teacher's keeping.

In keeping with = *in harmony;*   Your statement is in keeping with the rules.

Out of keeping = *against;*   Greg's description is out of keeping with the guidelines.

Kernel = *central, main point;*   This is the kernel of the policy.

Keep it up = *continue doing same;*   Ian is playing well. He should keep it up.

Keep aside = *keep out of the way;*   Keep this brick aside.

Keep on the track = *follow right way;*   Jim keeps himself on the track to get success in life.

A different kettle of fish = *a different thing or person;*   Rose is a different kettle of fish from other girls.

Out of key = *not in harmony;*   What you say is out of key with the rules.

Be keyed up = *look nervous, excited;*   When he saw the tiger from machan, he looked keyed up.

Keystone = *main theme;*   Economic development was the keystone of his speech.

Kick in the pants = *do extra efforts;*   If you want to win the match, you need a kick in the pants.

Kick in the teeth = *great setback;*   Lack of sponsors is a kick in the teeth of hockey.

Kick off = *begin, start;*   The World Cup will kick off soon.

Kick-start = *add further force;*   Good policies will kick-start our economy.

Live like a king = *live in comfort;*   He lives like a king.

Till kingdom come = *forever;* Good deeds live till kingdom come.

Bring to knees = *make weak, submissive;* Strong laws will bring all corrupt people to their knees.

Knee-jerk = *automatic;* The minister's remark created knee-jerk reaction in society.

The knives are out = *hostile situation;* The knives are out and the two countries are on the warpath.

Knife-edge = *tense situation;* The world is living on knife-edge.

Knight in shining armour = *a man who helps in difficulty;* Bob came as a knight in shining armour and saved the club.

Knock down = *break;* They knocked down the wall.

Knock off = *reduce price;* The shopkeeper knocked off Rs.50.

Knock out = *defeat, out of contest;* United Club has been knocked out of tournament.

Knock something out = *produce, finish;* Roy knocked out the book in two years.

Knock-back = *disappointments, rejection;* Everybody gets some knock-backs in life.

Be in the know = *have an idea, aware of;* I am in the know of this secret.

Know no bound = *unlimited;* Knowledge has no bounds.

Know-nothing = *ignorant person;* She is know-nothing.

Kick up a row = *create controversy;* The remark kicked up a row in parliament.

Killer instinct = *desire to defeat;* A team should have a killer instinct.

Beyond one's ken = *knowledge;* It is beyond my ken.

Keyword = *main point;* Quality is the keyword of our compaign.

Knotty points = *difficult;* These are the knotty points of this policy.

Keep the lid = *check, control;* Keep the lid on boiling public mood.

Keep in order = *systematic way;* Always keep your papers in order.

Kick out of doldrums = *take out of depression;* A good coach kicks the team out of doldrums.

Time lag = *time between two things;* There is a time lag between an interview and the result.

Lag behind = *remain backward;* Jane lags behind other students.

Lame duck = *unsuccessful man;* He is a lame duck for the team.

Land on one's feet = *become successful;* After facing many difficulties, he has landed on his feet.

A landmark = *important;* He delivered a landmark judgement.

Fall into lap = *come someone's way;* Victory fell into his lap.

In the lap of luxury = *live in comfort;* Dan lives in the lap of luxury.

At large = *not to be found;* The culprit is at large.

In large measure = *to a great limit;* Our success depends in large measure on our hard work.

On large scale = *covering large area;* The sale was organised on large scale.

Large-hearted = *liberal, open;* Ron is a large-hearted gentleman.

For a lark = *for fun;* We played for a lark.

Lash out = *hit, strike;* In his article, the writer lashed out at his critics.

As a last resort = *finally, ultimately;* As a last resort the wife will come back to her husband.

Latch on to = *remain fixed or attached;* Good companies latch on to good executives.

Larger than life = *undue, inappropriate;* We present larger than life picture of poverty.

A last ditch = *final act;* They made a last ditch effort to save his life.

A good laugh = *for fun;* We went to a park for a good laugh.

Laugh in the face = *show contempt, disrespect;* Criminals can laugh in the face of authorities.

No laughing matter = *a serious issue;* Terrorism is no laughing matter.

Lay claim to = *assert one's right;* He laid claim to his father's property.

Lay down the law = *make;* A good government lays down good laws.

Lay hand on = *possess, take;* The thief laid hands on everything he could find.

Lay open to = *expose;* You can lay yourself open to charges.

Lay aside = *keep away;* One should lay aside some money for old age.

Lay off = *give up;* I laid off this bad habit of chewing tobacco.

Lay up = *suffer from illness;* Ken was laid up with malaria.

Lead astray = *take a wrong path;* A mother never leads her children astray.

Lead by the nose = *in complete control;* Martha leads her husband by the nose.

Take the lead = *go ahead;* Sampras took the lead in the final set.

Lead from the front = *set example;* A captain of a team should lead from the front.

Leading light = *prominent person;* Scientists are the leading lights of the nation.

Leaf through = *read quickly;* She is leafing through the pages of the book.

In league with = *in agreement;* Cole was in league with the robbers.

In different league = *different type;* Sachin and Lara are in different league with other batsmen.

Leave in the cold = *helpless;* His friend has left him in the cold.

Thin line = *little difference;* There is a thin line between superstition and faith.

Lack soul = *weak, lifeless;* These ideas are old and lack soul.

Loads of blessings = *many;* The newly married couple received loads of blessings.

Laugh out = *unwelcome, rejected;* He was laughed out of the USA.

Loom over = *hang over, face;* A controversy is looming over the book.

Line up = *arrange, present;* Bell will line up a battery of lawyers.

Leap in the dark = *unpredictable step;* This action is only a lead in the dark.

Leapfrog = *take advantageous position;* Ron has leapfrogged into a cosy situation.

A new lease of life = *better prospects;* More loans will give a new lease of life to the company.

Leave much to be desired = *unsatisfactory;* Your work leaves much to be desired.

Leech on = *take away, exploit;* He leeches off the workers' hard labour.

Not have a leg to stand on = *without sound reason;* The statement has no leg to stand on.

At length = *in detail;* Tell me at length the whole thing.

Lend an ear = *listen to;* Please lend an ear to my advice.

Let-off = *chance to avoid defeat;* We had three let-offs but we won the match.

A level playing field = *get fair chance;* The government should provide a level playing field to all companies.

On a level with = *equal to;* Students can't be on a level with a teacher.

Give leverage = *power, clout;* Local bodies should be given leverage for the development of a town.

Take liberty = *behave in improper way;* Don't take liberty with your parents.

Lick boots = *behave in servile way to gain favour;* The greedy person can lick your boots.

Lick into shape = *make fitter, stronger;* The physical instructor is licking the boys into shape.

Lick one's wounds = *recover confidence;* After its defeat the party is licking its wounds.

In lieu of = *in place of;* I'll give you a book in lieu of a book.

Throw a lifeline = *save someone;* Ann was in difficulty and her mother threw a lifeline to her.

See the light of the day = *come into reality;* The policy could not see the light of the day.

Make light of = *consider unimportant;* Don't make light of a scientist's work.

In limbo = *in neglected state;* The scheme is in limbo.

All down the line = *at every stage;* He is a careless boy all down the line.

Bring into line = *bring in conformity;* The new economic policy will bring the country into line with other countries.

The end of the line = *no further progress possible;* I will not help you anymore. You have reached the end of the line.

In line with = *according to, like;* The salary we give is in line with other institutions.

Out of line = *disproportionate, not like;* The product is out of line with its reputation.

Line one's pocket = *make money dishonestly;* The contractor is lining his pocket.

Lionise someone = *pay extra attention;* Cricketers are lionised in our country.

Live off = *depend;* Maya does not live off her husband.

Live for = *regard as very important;* He lives for his family.

Live through = *survive, pass through;* Some live through very hard times.

Live up to = *fulfil;* One should live up to one's reputation and dignity.

Lock horns with = *in conflict with;* Some countries lock horns with other countries.

Lock, stock and barrel = *totally;* The boys have left the hostel lock, stock and barrel.

In the long run = *finally;* In the long run a hard working man succeeds.

The long and short of it = *all which can be said;* The long and short of it is that you are good.

Long haul = *tough work;* To enforce this law is a long haul.

Look through (somebody) = *ignore;* Cliff looked through me.

Look through (something) = *read;* We looked through the book.

Look into = *investigate;* The authorities looked into his past records.

Look in the eye = *look directly;* The policeman looked in the eye of the culprit.

Look the other way = *ignore;* They look the other way at the corruption.

Look to the future = *plan for future;* The students should look to the future.

Look-alike = *a closely resembling person;* He is a Richard look-alike.

On the lookout for = *search for;* We are on the lookout for the tiger.

Loom large = *threatening to happen;* Terrorism is looming large everywhere.

In the loop = *know, aware of;* The minister is in the loop of this disaster.

Lordly air = *show pomp, greatness;* King William blew a lordly air about himself.

Loose cannon = *person causing damage;* Don't tell this secret to him. He is a loose cannon.

Lose face = *become less respectable;* He has lost election and lost face.

Lose heart = *become disappointed, discouraged;* Henry has lost heart after his failure.

Fight a losing battle = *a fight ending in failure;* They are fighting a losing battle against corruption.

Lost cause = *a thing that can't succeed;* The fight against AIDS is becoming a lost cause.

Lotus-eater = *pleasure-loving but impractical;* Alice is a lotus-eater.

As luck would have it = *because of chance;* As luck would have it, I saw a beautiful leopard in the forest.

A lump in the throat = *sad feeling;* His poor condition left a lump in the pastor's throat.

Leave in the lurch = *in difficulty;* I am sure Ken will not leave me in the lurch.

Lynx-eyed = *has keen sight;* He is healthy and is lynx-eyed.

Real Mc Coy = *real thing;*   Your dishonesty turned out to be the real Mc Coy.

Macroscopic analysis = *visible;*   The article gives a macroscopic analysis of our society.

Far from the madding crowd = *away;*   The saint lived far from the madding crowd.

Made to measure = *according to size;*   The shirt has been made to your measure.

A maelstrom = *place of confusion;*   Bus stations are maelstroms of passengers.

Main line = *main route;*   This place is a main line of drug trafficking.

Mainspring = *main part;*   The theory was the mainspring of capitalism.

Make up mind = *decide;*   You should make up your mind to go to school.

Make way = *make room for others;*   We should make way for the young generation.

Make for = *go, move;*   I am making for home.

Make something of = *understand;* John made nothing of what his teacher said.

Make off with = *carry away, steal;* The thief made off with her ornaments.

Kiss and make up = *reconcile, friendly;* Now let's kiss and make up.

Make-believe = *imaginary;* They live in a make-believe world.

Makeshift = *temporary;* We lived in makeshift tents after the flood.

Make haste = *work fast;* Make haste or you will miss the train.

Make headway = *progress;* The scheme is not making any headway.

Make it a point = *always remember;* Make it a point that you will work sincerely.

In the making = *being prepared;* The plan is in the making.

As one man = *everybody together;* We will fight against terrorism as one man.

Make a man out of someone = *teach, train;* I will make man out of you and you will be a doctor.

The man in the street = *ordinary man;* A good leader cares for the man in the street.

Man of action = *practical;* Napoleon was a man of action.

Man of honour = *of right action and conduct;* A man of honour will not do this disgraceful thing.

Man of letters = *great writer;* Tagore was a man of letters.

Man of the moment = *important person of a time;* During World War II, Churchill proved to be man of the moment.

Man of straw = *a bogus person;* Dean is not a man of straw.

To a man = *without exception;* They will support you to a man.

A good many = *a large number of people;* A good many of us believe in economic reforms.

Manyfold = *by many times;* It will increase the problem manyfold.

Many-sided = *many sides, aspects;* Poverty has many-sided reasons.

Map out = *prepare;* Map out your plan for the future.

Put on the map = *make famous;* 'Gitanjali' put Tagore on the world map.

Wipe off the map = *remove;* Let us wipe corruption off the map.

On the march = *moving;* The army is on the march.

Mad as a March hare = *absolutely insane;* He is as mad as a March hare.

Margin of error = *small mistake;* There should not be a margin of error in our work.

Marginalise = *leave as unimportant;* The group has been marginalised by the company.

Get off the mark = *get ready;* The test is round the corner. Let us get off the mark.

Leave a mark = *leave significant effect;* Gandhiji has left his mark on the world.

Mark time = *wait for opportunity;*   Abe is marking his time and will join the group later on.

Close to the mark = *nearly accurate;*   You are close to the mark.

Off the mark = *inaccurate;*   His answer is way off the mark.

On the mark = *correct;*   What you say is on the mark.

Up to the mark = *up to the standard;*   Their work is up to the mark.

On the market = *available;*   The new watch will be on the market soon.

Hit the market = *available for sale;*   The book will hit the market next month.

To the marrow = *fully;*   I was frightened to the marrow.

Man of the masses = *very popular;*   He is a man of the masses.

Meet one's match = *meet one's equal;*   Roy will meet his match in Ron.

Matinee idol = *handsome actor;*   Dev Anand was a matinee idol.

Mean business = *realistic, earnest;* Don't talk unnecessarily. I mean business.

Beyond means = *beyond one's income;*   It is a costly shirt and beyond my means.

By all means = *certainly;*   You can talk to me by all means.

By no means = *in no way, not at all;*   Our victory is by no means possible.

Beyond measure = *to a great extent;*   He troubles me beyond measure.

Easy meat = *an easy prey, victim;* An inexperienced batsman is an easy prey of a good bowler.

Megabuck = *a lot of money;* Reputed companies are earning megabucks.

One's mentor = *guru, teacher;* He was Pat's political mentor.

Go on one's merry way = *go on without thinking of consequences;* He went on his merry way and spoilt his life.

Make merry = *enjoy with someone;* Pip is making merry with his friend.

Mess around = *act foolishly;* They are messing around in the kitchen.

Mess up = *mishandle;* The government has messed up the political siutation.

Get the message = *get the signal;* The staff has got the message from the boss.

Send a message = *make clear;* We sent the message that corruption can't be tolerated.

Put on mettle = *test capability;* The board put the cadets on their mettle.

Middle ground = *a ground of compromise;* He takes the middle ground in face of opposition.

Middle-of-the-road = *moderate position;* The government adopts middle-of-the-road policy.

Midsummer madness = *stupid behaviour;* George is down with midsummer madness.

In midstream = *in the middle;* I was giving my statement and he stopped me in midstream.

Miles ahead = *far advance;*   She is miles ahead of the girls.

In milk = *producing milk;*   The cow is in milk.

A million dollars = *extremely good;*   It is a million dollar question.

In two minds = *undecided, uncertain;*   I could not go because I was in two minds.

Come to mind = *occur;*   This idea came to my mind.

Have a mind of one's own = *independent;*   Jim has a mind of his own.

Mind one's P's and Q's = *behave properly;*   When in school, children should mind their P's and Q's.

On someone's mind = *preoccupied by problems;*   There are many problems on my mind.

Out of one's mind = *out of control;*   Ivan is out of his mind.

Mind-blowing = *very impressive;*   The Taj Mahal is really a mind-blowing monument.

Mind-boggling = *causing surprise;*   It is a mind-boggling question.

Give a miss = *not to use or take;*   There were many things to eat, but we gave them a miss.

Miss the bus = *fail to use an opportunity;*   Zen offered me a job but I missed the bus.

Missionary zeal = *do with commitment, dedication;*   Do your work with missionary zeal.

Get mixed up in = *involve in dubious dealing;*   Jack got mixed up in a fraud.

A mix up = *confusion;*   There was a mix up between the two batsmen.

Mixed bag = *neither good nor bad;* Our tour proved to be a mixed bag of success.

Mixed economy = *including private and state sector;* We believe in mixed economy.

Make a mockery of = *laugh or tease at;* Corruption is makng a mockery of our democracy.

Media mogul = *powerful person;* Editors are media moguls.

Money talks = *money gives power;* In our age, money talks.

Money-grubbing = *eager to get money;* Dubious people carry on money-grubbing operations.

Money-spinner = *which gives profit;* Media industry is a money-spinner.

Make a monkey of = *cheat and humiliate;* He made a monkey of me.

Monkey business = *ridiculous thing;* Stop this monkey business in the class.

Moolah = *money, profit;* Corporate houses aim at moolah.

Over the moon = *very happy;* She won first prize and was over the moon.

Moonshine = *impractical, foolish idea;* These views are moonshine.

Mother wit = *common sense;* One should have mother wit.

Give mouth = *say loudly;* Give mouth to what you say.

On the move = *make progress;* The new plan is on the move.

Muddle-headed = *confused;*   He is a muddle-headed young man.

Mud-slinging = *use insults and charges;*   A mud-slinging match is going on between the two parties.

Without a murmur = *without complaint;*   Bob does his work without a murmur.

Mushroom growth = *great development;*   There is a mushroom growth of economic development.

Myriad-minded = *very great;*   Newton was a myriad-minded genius.

Aura of mystery = *a quality difficult to understand;*   There is an aura of mystery about him.

Mover and shaker = *change something;*   She is known as a mover and shaker in the party.

Masterful account = *wonderful description;*   He gave a masterful account of society.

Mass of ignorance = *foolish, stupid;*   This mob is a mass of ignorance.

Make to = *reach, occupy;*   Women are making to the top jobs.

Make a pitch for = *find, seek;*   The US is making a pitch for good Indian students.

Anxious moments = *worrying;*   France had some anxious moments in the first half of the football match.

Make-or-break = *do or die, hard;*   It was a make-or-break day for the German team.

Match the time = *move with;*   You should match the time and demand.

Reach the nadir = *lowest point;*   During the Second World War the world economy reached the nadir.

Nagging question = *difficult question;*   Terrorism is a nagging question for the world.

Fight tooth and nail = *with determination;*   We will fight tooth and nail.

Nail biting = *very tense, exciting;*   It was a nail-biting match.

Catch napping = *find unprepared;*   The goalkeeper was caught napping.

Go native = *adopt other country;*   Cook settled in Australia and went native.

Natty = *smart;*   You are a natty dresser.

Against nature = *unethical, immoral;*   It is against nature to kill animals.

Come to naught = *proved useless;*   All my efforts to correct him came to naught.

Knotty problem = *difficult;*   It is really a knotty problem.

Near at hand = *very close;*   Your interview is near at hand.

Nearest and dearest = *close relatives;*   Kip's nearest and dearest have been informed.

Near-death experience = *out of body experience;*   He told me of his near-death experience.

Near miss = *a narrow escape;*   I had a near miss when I fell down from a rock.

Have the neck to do = *show disrespect;*   He had the neck to enter the principal's room.

Neck and neck = *very close;*   They are running neck and neck.

Break-neck speed = *very fast;*   He was driving at break-neck speed.

In need = *require help;*   We are in need of money.

Do the needful = *do what is required;*   Pip is a poor boy. Please do the needful for him.

Needy person = *a man who requires help;*   She is a needy person.

Needle in a haystack = *impossible to find out;*   To see a snow leopard is as difficult as to find a needle in a haystack.

In the neighbourhood = *around;*   The cost of this project will be in the neighbourhood of Rs two crore.

Nerk = *foolish person;*   He is a nerk.

A bundle of nerves = *a timid person;*   Shane is a bundle of nerves.

Get on nerves = *annoy or angry;*   She gets on her brother's nerves.

Have nerves of steel = *brave, courageous;*   Ron has nerves of steel.

Live on nerves = *anxious, tense;*   Her father is ill and she lives on her nerves.

Strain every nerve = *make great efforts;* The players strained every nerve to win the match.

War of nerves = *use psychological means for victory;* The two countries are waging a war of nerves.

Nerve centre = *place that controls;* Mumbai is the nerve centre of the Indian share market.

Net profit = *achieve, get;* The company netted a huge profit.

Slip through the net = *escape;* The thief slipped through the net of the police.

Graph the nettle = *face a problem boldly;* If you graph the nettle, you will succeed in life.

Never-ending = *have no end;* It is a never-ending dispute.

New-fashioned = *novel, new;* It is a new-fashioned idea.

In the news = *get publicity;* She is in the news today.

Next in line = *next to succeed;* You are next in line to the post.

The next world = *after death;* We know nothing of the next world.

To a nicety = *exactly;* Bill does his job to a nicety.

In good nick = *good condition;* Brian Lara is in good nick.

In the nick of time = *in time;* We reached in the nick of time.

Night is closing in = *approaching;* The night is closing in and you should go home.

Fall like nine pins = *be defeated;* The enemy fell like nine pins.

Nit-picking = *fault finding;* Bartha has nit-picking habits.

No two ways about it = *sure;*   It is true. There are no two ways about it.

Of no account = *worthless;*   Maya is of no account.

Of no consequence = *unimportant;*   This statement is of no consequence.

Noble lineage = *of high family;*   Charles is of noble lineage.

In no way = *not at all;*   In no way can I help you.

A nodding acquaintance = *some knowledge;*   Children should have a nodding acquaintance with computer.

Be on nodding terms = *little familiar;*   Rex is on nodding terms with Rock.

Get the nod = *get approval, okay;*   The project got the nod from the government.

No go = *prove useless;*   I tried to save his life but it was a no go.

Non-event = *fail to happen;*   The plan remained a non-event.

No-nonsense approach = *real, sensible;*   Parents should adopt a no-nonsense approach towards their children.

A nose for = *aptitude, liking;*   The boy has a nose for good books.

Nose ahead = *go ahead;*   He is nosing ahead of other competitors.

Nose into = *interfere;*   Please don't nose into my work.

By a nose = *narrowly;*   I won the race by a nose.

Give a bloody nose = *defeat;*   The army gave a bloody nose to the enemy.

Take a nosedive = *fall;*   The prices took a nosedive.

Keep nose out of = *not to interfere;* Keep your nose out of my business.

Under the nose = *in full view;* The crime took place under the nose of the police.

Notch up = *get, achieve;* We notched up a fine victory.

Note down = *write;* I noted down the sentence.

Hit the right note = *say right;* A wise man always hits the right note.

Of note = *important;* He is a scientist of note.

Take note of = *be attentive to;* An administrator should take note of the problems.

Noted for = *known for, famous;* The school is noted for its high standard.

For nothing = *free, without payment;* Jill is teaching for nothing.

At short notice = *within little time;* You can be dismissed at short notice.

Put on notice = *warn;* All parties have been put on notice about it.

Notwithstanding the fact that = *despite the fact;* Notwithstanding the fact that he lived in poverty, he made many discoveries.

Now and then = *from time to time;* Mac comes here now and then.

Now or never = *absolutely important;* It is now or never, you will have to pass the test.

Come nowhere = *below standard;* Our athletes come nowhere near the world standard.

From nowhere = *come suddenly;* The man-eating tiger came from nowhere and killed the man.

No-win situation = *success is impossible;* We have reached a no-win situation in football World Cup.

A nitwit = *stupid person;* Neil is a nitwit.

Not to one's liking = *according to taste;* Your views are not to my liking.

Not up to the mark = *according to standard;* Your work is not up to the mark.

A non-starter = *which fails to begin;* The project remained a non-starter.

Nub of the problem = *central point;* This is the nub of the issue.

Norms and nuances = *subtle points;* English language has its own norms and nuances.

Nucleus = *crux, important part;* The Gandhi family is the nucleus of the Congress party.

Nurse a grievance = *bear grudge;* He should not nurse a grievance against you.

Nuts and bolts = *basics, fundamentals;* These are the nuts and bolts of banking system.

Off nut = *crazy, mad;* Tony is off his nut.

A tough nut = *strong and difficult person;* This economic adviser is a tough nut.

Make one nuts = *make crazy, mad;* Now stop. You have made me nuts.

In a nutshell = *in brief;* Tell me your story in a nutshell.

One's nightmare = *great problem;*   Castro is the US's worst nightmare.

Hard-nosed policy = *realistic;*   A country should have a hard-nosed foreign policy.

Keep one's nose out = *stay away;*   Jack should keep his nose out of my business.

Get into nitty-gritty = *know intricacies;*   Tom should get into the nitty-gritty of this issue.

Nip in the bud = *kill in the beginning;*   We should nip all bad habits in the bud.

Carve a niche = *become famous;*   He carved a niche for himself in world history.

A driving need = *want badly;*   She has a driving need to get to the top.

Bug someone no end = *to trouble, irritate;*   You bug me no end.

No hope in hell = *have no chance, hope;*   Mercy has no hope in hell.

Lose one's nerve = *feel upset;*   Never lose your nerve in any situation.

Have no clue = *to know nothing;*   I have no clue about Jim.

Every nook and cranny = *from every part;*   They represent every nook and cranny of society.

Oasis of peace = *a peaceful place;*   This place is an oasis of peace.

Feels one's oats = *feel happy, lively;*   Neil is feeling his oats now.

Under oath = *take oath to tell the truth;*   He is under oath and will tell the truth.

In obedience to = *according to;*   We removed him from the post in obedience to our policy.

Pay obeisance to = *pay respect;*   He paid obeisance to the king.

Object lesson = *an example;*   This punishment is an object lesson to all students.

Under obligation = *duty bound;*   Good citizens are under obligation to follow the law.

Pass into oblivion = *become extinct;*   The old customs are fast passing into oblivion.

Slide into obscurity = *become unimportant;*   Good work will not slide into obscurity.

Under observation = *to be watched closely;*   Your behaviour is under observation.

Keen observer = *who watches keenly;* Dickens was a keen observer of human society.

On occasion = *from time to time;* Bell comes here on occasion.

Rise to the occasion = *do better than expected;* Sam rose to the occasion and scored two goals.

Occupational hazard = *professional risk;* Fishermen face occupational hazards.

Out of one's depth = *lack knowledge;* Hogg failed to do this work, because he was out of his depth.

Out of sync = *not on good terms;* Watson is out of sync with his captain and coach.

Over the hill = *no more effective;* Some bowlers are over the hill now.

Give brush-off = *rebuke, insult;* The boss gave me the brush-off.

Get something off the ground = *start, begin;* The company wants this plan to get off the ground.

On the horizon = *come up, appear;* New technology is now on the horizon.

Open one's door = *allow to enter;* India is opening its doors to multinational companies.

Down and out = *dejected, defeated;* After the debacle, the party is down and out.

Out of the race = *no more in contention;* Dick is out of the race now.

Out of sorts = *unhappy, dull;* Yes, I am feeling out of sorts today.

No object = *no restriction, influence;* For a wise man power is no object.

Raise objection = *disapproval;* Tim raised many objections to my views.

At odds = *in conflict;* This idea is at odds with my policy.

By all odds = *in every way;* I will help you by all odds.

In the offing = *appear soon, come;* Good plans and policies are in the offing.

As old as the hills = *very old;* Pyramids are as old as the hills.

Hold an olive branch = *a peace offer;* They held out an olive branch to the enemy.

On and on = *talk continuously;* He went on and on about his past achievements.

Open with = *very frank, open;* Mark is open with me.

Open-door policy = *free;* Most of the countries follow an open-door policy.

Open to all = *free, without restriction;* The college is open to all students.

Give an opening = *chance, opportunity;* Good business houses give an opening to dashing executives.

Of the opinion = *believe, maintain;* We are of the opinion that God is everywhere.

Grab the opportunity = *take, accept;* Always grab the opportunity with both hands.

In opposition = *contrary;* Your views are in opposition to my ideas.

Opt out = *not to participate;*   Europe is opting out of the treaty.

Send into orbit = *make happy, excited;*   Their victory in the World Cup sent them into orbit.

Well-orchestrated voice = *with desired effect;*   The leaders spoke in a well-orchestrated voice.

Out for = *to get, achieve;*   Brian is out for a good job.

Out of reach = *beyond reach;*   Luxuries are out of a poor man's reach.

In outline = *is broad terms;*   The policies have been agreed in outline.

Out of date = *irrelevant, old;*   These ideas are now out of date.

Be over = *no more affected;*   Fortunately, we are now over the trouble.

Owe something to = *because of something;*   I owe all my achievement to hard work.

Owe a grudge = *have animosity, jealousy;*   A good man never owes a grudge against a poor man.

Come into one's own = *become aware;*   Neil was feeling giddy, but soon came into his own.

On one's own = *alone, without others;*   Reid went to the town on his own.

Own up = *admit, accept;*   We should own up our mistakes.

Send someone packing = *make a person leave;*   If you don't follow my order, I will send you packing.

Pack someone off = *send without warning;*   The principal packed off the boy to his house.

Paddle one's own canoe = *be independent;*   Sam is now paddling his own canoe.

Go down the pan = *a failure;*   All my efforts went down the pan.

On the spur of the moment = *instantly;*   On the spur of the moment he decided to fight the election.

Out of hand = *no more in control;*   The whole issue has gone out of hand.

Out of this world = *wonderful, fine;*   This design is absolutely out of this world.

An ocean of = *on large scale, large quantity;*   Bill has oceans of money.

Odd job = *a casual work;*   He is doing odd jobs.

The odds = *chances;*   The odds are in your favour.

Live on the edge = *precarious, risky;*   People of the west generally live on the edge.

Ready for the off = *ready to go;*   My work is over and I am ready for the off.

Off and on = *now and then;*   He comes here off and on.

Off the mark = *away from target;*   What you state is wide off the mark.

Look offbeat = *unusual, not normal;*   Harry looks offbeat today.

Off colour = *unwell;*   Jason is feeling off colour today.

Give offence to someone = *insult, resentment;*   She never gives offence to children.

On the offensive = *aggressive;*   The rival team is on the offensive.

Off the record = *unofficial;*   He made an off the record statement.

Off the cuff = *without prethinking;*   The minister made an off the cuff statement.

On offer = *present, available;*   Some goods are on offer.

Offhand = *without previous thought;*   I can't write this offhand.

Off-key = *inappropriate, wrong;*   Your remark is off-key.

Off-price = *sell below normal price;*   There is an off-price sale.

Oil the wheels = *make smooth;*   Good friends oil the wheels of our life.

Work like well-oiled machine = *move smoothly;*   The team is playing like a well-oiled machine.

Old guard = *old person averse to change;*   Ashley is an old guard.

Old-wive's tale = *incorrect belief;*   What Ben says is an old-wive's tale.

Olive branch = *a peace offer;*   Dean's critics are now holding an olive branch.

Olympian height = *high position;*   He has reached an Olympian height.

Alpha and Omega = *beginning and end;*   God is alpha and omega.

Ill omen = *a portent of bad thing;*   The black cat is an ill omen.

On the move = *progress, do well;*   The project is on the move.

On the track = *moving on right line;* The policy is on the track.

On the wrong track = *result in failure;* The economy is on the wrong track.

Keep track of = *know about something;* Keep track of the enemy's movements.

On line = *in danger;* My career and life are on line.

On good terms = *friendly;* Colins is on good terms with me.

On the whole = *finally;* The situation on the whole is bad.

On the target = *accurate, right;* The bowler was bang on the target.

On to something = *know, discover;* Your teacher is on to your mischief.

Ongoing = *continuing, in operation;* Don't disturb this ongoing scheme.

At once = *immediately;* Hall went away at once.

Once and for all = *finally, last time;* I told Kemp once and for all that he could lose his job.

Once in a while = *occasionally;* Stella comes here once in a while.

Get in one = *understand soon, quickly;* Smith is intelligent and gets the things in one.

One-man = *done by one man;* It is a one-man work.

In one piece = *perfectly, fine;* Oliver fell from the cliff but came out in one piece.

Have one-track mind = *concerned with one thing;* Kip has one-track mind.

Know one's onions = *know something thoroughly;* He is a good science teacher and knows his onions.

Have oodles = *possess in large number;* Tyson has oodles of money.

To be open with = *frank;* Ruth is open with her friends.

Open the door to = *allow;* We have opened the door to multinational companies.

Keep open house = *welcome the visitors;* My mother always kept an open house.

Opinionated person = *arrogant, stubborn;* William is an opinionated person.

A matter of opinion = *an unproven thing;* Whether life exists after death is a matter of opinion.

Optical illusion = *not in existence;* To see water in the desert is an optical illusion.

An optimist = *a person who believes in bright future;* One should always be an optimist.

Have no option = *no other choice;* I have no other option, so I accept this job.

Keep options open = *remain uncommitted;* A far-sighted man keeps his options open.

Opt out of something = *not to take part;* Europe opted out of this agreement.

On the rise = *when something is in the air;* Catch the ball on the rise.

In order = *appropriate, correct;* The work he did was in order.

In order that = *so that, with a view to;*   We read books in order that we make our life better.

In order to = *with the aim, so that;*   They work hard in order to get success.

On order = *on request;*   He prepared the cake on order.

Out of order = *in chaos, not working;*   My radio is out of order.

Under order = *receive instructions;*   I am under order not to tell about it.

Order of the day = *a common thing;*   Corruption has become the order of the day.

Out of the ordinary = *uncommon, silly;*   A test batsman should not do anything out of the ordinary.

Ornamental style = *full of beauty and grace;*   He writes in ornamental style.

Give new orientation = *direction, dynamism;*   Burke gave new orientation to this theory.

Feel out of the game = *feel upset, defeated;*   I can't solve this puzzle. I am feeling out of the game.

Out-of-the-box thinking = *open, broad ideas;*   To solve the Kashmir problem, we need out-of-the-box thinking.

Get out of the way = *remove, keep away;*   Get Jill out of the way.

On the learning curve = *in the process of learning;*   Children are on the learning curve.

An ostrich = *unable to face reality;*   Mac is an ostrich. He lives in a make-believe world.

At outs = *in dispute, conflict;*   Collins was at outs with his friends.

Out to do = *ready, keen;*   I am out to tell him the reality.

Out and out = *completely, absolutely;*   Adam Smith was out and out an economist.

An outside chance = *little, remote;*   Our party has an outside chance to win the election.

Go into overdrive = *do excessive work;*   The advertising agency went into overdrive to get public attention.

Oxygen of publicity = *help, assistance;*   The product requires oxygen of publicity.

Offer the ultimate = *provide the best thing;*   The hotel offers the ultimate in food.

P

Go to the pack = *get destroyed, defunct;* All my plan went to the pack.

Pack with punch = *fill with power, effective;* His statement was packed with punch.

Painstaking efforts = *great, complete;* Darwin made painstaking efforts to discover it.

Paint the town red = *enjoy exessively;* The victorious team has come and is painting the town red.

Come within the pale = *limits, parameters;* His behaviour does not come within the pale of society.

Palmy day = *happy, successful;* I remember the palmy days of the past.

Push the panic button = *require immediate help;* Europe is pushing panic button on the issue of terrorism.

Above par = *better;* The work is above par.

On a par = *equal;* Both the countries are on a par.

Paragon of perfection = *an example;* The product is a paragon of perfection.

Man of parts = *an able person;* The economist is a man of parts.

Parting shot = *final remark made at departure;* Don't come again was her parting shot.

A passe = *no more in fashion;* This style is a passe now.

A passport to = *thing ensuring success;* Hard work is a passport to success.

A pat on the back = *receive applause;* Ben got a pat on the back by his father.

A rich talent pool = *a source of talents;* Our organisation is a rich talent pool of executives.

Progressive work culture = *good system;* We believe in progressive work culture.

At the top of the pyramid = *in the top section;* Make changes at the top of the pyramid.

Patch up = *establish peace, harmony;* Dorris patched up the differences between her brothers.

Pave the way for = *create situation;* His brilliant century paved the way for our victory.

At peace = *friendly, calm;* Neil is a peace with his neighbours.

Make peace with = *get reconciled;* The party is making peace with the opposition.

At the peak = *at the highest point;* The tourist season is at the peak.

Panic station = *alarming state;* We were at panic station because of the cyclone.

Panoptic view = *complete view;* The hill gives you a panoptic view of the valley.

Pare down = *cut off, reduce;* The producers have pared down the supply.

Par excellence = *better than others;* He is a designer par excellence.

Hold parley = *conference, meeting;* They are holding parley on border issue.

Parry question = *evade, avoid;* The diplomat parried questions asked by journalists.

Part company = *leave, go separately;* Evans has parted company with his old friend.

In every particular = *completely;* He knows his job in every particular.

Be a party to = *involved in;* Keans is a party to this deal.

Come to pass = *happen, occur;* It came to pass that he had given me some money.

Pass the baton = *give the responsibility;* Before he retired he passed the baton to his son.

Pass off = *happen, occur;* The time passed off peacefully.

In passing = *briefly;* He mentioned your name in passing.

Passionate about = *keen, anxious;* Lucy is passionate about poetry.

Past one's prime = *get old;* The tigress of Champawat was past her prime.

Past master = *expert, experienced;* Grant is past master at cheating others.

Not a patch on = *unequal, inferior;* Bob is not a patch on Bewan.

Lose patience = *get angry;*   Whenever he talks, he loses patience.

Pathetic performance = *poor, sad;*   Joy's performance was pathetic.

Give pause for thought = *think carefully;*   Our rival's superb performance gives us pause for thought.

Go pear shaped = *go wrong;*   During war time, economy goes pear shaped.

Peg out = *mark;*   They peg out the area of the ground.

Pell-mell = *seen in confusion;*   The children ran pell-mell.

Pencil thin = *very slim;*   My daughter is pencil thin.

Penny plain = *simple;*   The new book is penny plain.

A people person = *social and friendly;*   Elis is a people person.

To be peppered with = *using liberally;*   The book is peppered with quotations.

Peppy advertisement = *energetic, lively;*   It is a peppy advertisement.

At one's peril = *at great risk;*   Jones is going on an expedition at his own peril.

Perilous position = *full of danger;*   Save him from this perilous position.

Perk something up = *make lively;*   Dona perked the atmosphere up.

Put into perspective = *right position, relationship;*   Put your views into right perspective.

A Pharisee = *conceited, hypocrite;*   Fred is a Pharisee.

In phases = *in stages, harmony;*   The plan is being implemented in phases.

Photo-finish = *close contest;*   The race ended in a photo-finish.

Photogenic face = *attractive, smart;*   She has a photogenic face.

Pick holes in = *find fault;*   We pick holes in other's work.

Pick a fight = *quarrel;*   He picked a fight with me.

Pick through = *find out something;*   The poor children are picking through the garbage.

A pickup = *increase;*   There is a pickup in milk consumption.

Have one's pick = *choice;*   You can have your pick from these items.

Pigeon-hearted = *timid, weak;*   Barbara is pigeon-hearted.

In pawn = *held as security;*   All my belongings are in pawn.

Pawn off = *pass off, give;*   The cunning trader pawns off junk stuff on us.

Pay off = *give good results;*   Jim's hard work finally paid off.

Something peachy = *attractive;*   The surroundings are peachy.

Peal out = *give, pass on;*   They pealed out the news to the people.

Keep your pecker up = *be happy;*   Dick always keeps his pecker up.

Peel out = *go quickly;*   When he heard it, he peeled out.

Peerless performance = *unmatched, unequalled;* Diana gave a peerless performance.

Without peer = *incomparable, matchless;* Gilchrist is a wicket keeper without peer.

Pension off = *remove, dismissed;* The old peon has been pensioned off from job.

In penury = *poverty;* He died in penury.

Knock off perch = *remove from superior position;* Cooper will knock all industrialists off their perch.

To perfection = *perfectly;* Smith does his work to perfection.

In peril = *at risk, in danger;* The Republican party is in peril.

Pep talk = *to make courageous;* We should pep talk to the children.

In perpetuity = *forever;* Slavery has been banished in perpetuity.

In person = *personally;* You should meet him in person.

Pretty and petite = *attractive;* Simi is a pretty and petite girl.

Be piled with = *filled with;* George's room is piled up with books.

Make a pile = *make money;* He is doing a roaring business and is making a pile.

Pile up = *increase;* The orders for the book are piling up.

From pillar to post = *from one place to another;* Sam is running from pillar to post for a job.

Pin hopes on = *depend heavily;* Finally, we all pin our hopes on God.

Pin down = *defeat;*   The boxer pinned him down in two minutes.

Pioneering discovery = *new;*   She made pioneering discovery in the field of medicine.

Pip at the post = *defeat finally;*   Jack pipped Jim at the post.

Pipe dream = *something unattainable;*   Your plan will always be a pipe dream.

In the pipeline = *in the process of development;*   Many plans are in the pipeline.

Piping hot (food) = *very hot;*   My father eats piping hot food.

In a fit of pique = *in irritation;*   She left the hall in a fit of pique.

Piss off = *go away;*   Now you piss off.

A pitched battle = *tough, difficult;*   The army is engaged in a pitched battle.

Pitch for = *try to get, obtain;*   They are pitching for Chartsworth as a coach.

Play a pivotal role = *key, important;*   He played a pivotal role in our victory.

Plain as day = *very simple, clear;*   This is plain as day.

On one's plate = *occupied with work;*   I have a lot of work on my plate.

On a platter = *get something without efforts;*   The player got the chance on a platter.

Make a play of = *highlight something to gain prestige;*   They made a play of their new product.

Play by the rules = *follow right ways;* We always play by the rules.

The pick of = *the best thing, choice;* He is the pick of the selectors.

Pick up = *increase;* The storm has picked up.

No picnic = *difficult thing;* This job is no picnic, my friend.

Pierce someone's heart = *affect deeply;* The news of his death has pierced my heart.

One's pigeon = *duty, responsibility;* To look after the children is your pigeon.

Feel the pinch = *face difficulty;* As my business has failed, I feel the pinch.

Pine for = *desire, long for;* I pine for her love.

In the pink of = *very healthy;* Roma is in the pink of health.

Reach the pinnacle = *highest point;* He has reached the pinnacle of glory.

Pinpoint accuracy = *absolutely accurate;* He landed the plane with pinpoint accuracy.

Pit of despair = *shattered state;* Hector is in a pit of despair after his father's death.

Pit someone against = *set in competition;* They will pit Percy against Lucas in the election.

Plague with the problem = *face;* The society is plagued with the problem of corruption.

According to plan = *in a systemic way;* A successful man works according to a plan.

Keep one's feet planted on the ground = *realist, sensible;* It is better we keep our feet planted on the ground.

Plaster with = *cover with;* The wall is plastered with posters.

Play tricks on = *behave teasingly;* Some students play tricks on teachers.

Something plebeian = *unrefined;* He has a plebeian wife.

Play down something = *minimise, lessen;* Don't play down the gravity of the situation.

Play someone false = *cheat, deceive;* Harry plays his friends false.

Play into other's hands = *act on someone's will;* The husband plays into his wife's hands.

Play with fire = *take foolish steps;* He is spending his money recklessly and is playing with fire.

Play safe = *take no risk;* The team is playing safe.

A plethora of something = *excessively;* We have received a plethora of orders.

A plodder = *a person who works slowly;* Lew is a plodder.

Lose the plot = *lose ability to understand;* The team is losing the plot.

Plough through = *make progress slowly;* The child is ploughing through his lesson.

Plough a lonely furrow = *work alone;* He always ploughs a lonely furrow and succeeds.

Go down the plughole = *to be unsuccessful;* The project went down the plughole.

Plug the gap = *fill, cement;* Our defence is weak and we should plug the gap.

Plump salary = *fat, high;*   Good companies give plump salary.

Be a picture perfect = *beautiful;*   Indeed, Garbo was a picture perfect.

In the picture = *in the public notice;*   The writer is in the picture now.

Pass the buck = *pass the responsibility;*   He ran away and passed the buck on to me.

Pile up the pressure = *keep up the pressure;*   The pressure is piling up.

Do at one's own peril = *at one's own risk;*   You can do this work at your own peril.

Piggy back on someone = *take advantage;*   Politicians piggy back on the leader.

Put a damper on someone = *discourage;*   Don't put a damper on your friend.

At one's pleasure = *at one's wishes;*   He can dismiss you from the job at his pleasure.

Take pleasure = *get happiness;*   Children take pleasure from games.

In plenty = *in large quantity;*   There are books in plenty.

Plough up = *search, find out;*   Henry is ploughing up a hidden treasure.

Pluck up courage = *gather, get;*   Pluck up courage and face your enemy.

Plume on = *get satisfaction;*   Berty plumes himself on being a scientist.

Plumb for = *decide in favour of;*   I plumb for a cosy job.

Poach on other's territory = *encroach on other's right;* Colins encroaches on my territory.

In pocket = *very close, almost certain;* The match is in our pocket.

Out of pocket = *without money;* I can't help you. I am out of pocket.

Pocket an insult = *bear;* Jim pocketed an insult and remained calm.

Beside the point = *irrelevant;* What you say is beside the point.

Off the point = *unconnected, not related;* Here you are off the point.

Up to a point = *in some respect;* We may be right up to a point.

Poke fun at = *tease, mock, laugh at;* The children poke fun at the joker.

Up the pole = *crazy, mad;* His behaviour has driven me up the pole.

Take a poor view = *regard with disfavour;* Don't take a poor view of a serious situation.

Poppycock = *foolish, nonsense;* Ron talks poppycock.

A poser = *difficult, tricky question;* We are facing a poser.

Has loads of patience = *very calm;* Arnold has loads of patience.

Crack under pressure = *reveal the secret;* The culprit cracked under pressure.

Case in point = *an example;* His good work is a case in point.

Point of no return = *not to come back;*   Shaw has reached a point of no return.

Plumb new depths = *get worse;*   The problem has plumbed new depths.

No pushover = *difficult to handle;*   The player is very talented and no pushover.

Be puffed up = *become proud;*   Mills was never puffed up about his achievements.

In all one's puff = *in life;*   She remained calm in all her puff.

A publicity hound = *fond of publicity;*   The actress is a publicity hound.

Pull the plug = *stop, prevent;*   I pulled the plug on the agreement because it was not profitable.

Pull the strings = *in full control;*   The management is now pulling the strings.

Pull together = *work together;*   The captain and players should pull together.

Pull off = *achieve;*   The team pulled off a great surprise.

Pull out = *withdraw;*   We pulled out of the competition.

Pull up = *stop, halt;*   The train does not pull up here.

Plush area = *good;*   This is a plush area.

Pump up = *give improper support;*   You always pump up his pride.

As pleased as punch = *very jovial;*   The little boy is as pleased as punch.

Pure and simple = *nothing more;*   The batsman is out, pure and simple.

Hit a purple patch = *be successful, lucky;* The writer has hit a purple patch.

Get the push = *be dismissed from job;* If you don't work, you will get the push.

When push comes to shove = *commit oneself to a task;* When push comes to shove, he plays brilliantly.

Push ahead = *to proceed on;* He will push ahead with his plan.

Put it to = *challenge someone;* They put it down to Baker that he is a snob.

Put up or shut up = *either justify or remain quiet;* You should either put up or shut up.

Put back = *delay;* This bad policy will put back our plan.

Put down = *criticise, hit;* He puts me down everywhere.

Put through = *connect;* Please put me through to the manager.

Put something to = *submit, present;* Gary put up a good proposal.

Put up = *show, offer;* We put up a good fight.

Put up for = *offer for sale;* The company put up these watches for sale.

Put up with = *bear, tolerate;* He can't put up wih me

Puzzle out = *solve;* The girl puzzled out this problem.

Power ahead = *go forcefully;* Cynthia powered ahead of her rival.

Post-haste = *soon, immediately;* They came post-haste to meet their father.

On the prowl = *move about;*   The tiger is on the prowl.

Prime time = *main, important;*   Do telecast the programme on prime time.

Pry away = *take away;*   They pry away good workers from other organisations.

Of proven worth = *having good qualities;*   This surgeon is of proven worth.

Peel away = *take away;*   They are trying to peel him away from Communist party.

At a premium = *in great demand;*   This land is at a premium.

At premium price = *high;*   We purchased this property at premium price.

New brand in portfolio = *in the range of products;*   This camera is a new brand in the company's portfolio.

Pig out = *eat voraciously;*   We will pig out this delicious food.

Take pressure off = *lessen;*   Europe will take the pressure off USA.

Pump in = *score;*   Ronaldo pumped in a fantastic goal.

Hard part = *difficult thing;*   The hard part is to judge customers' mood.

Diverse platforms = *different departments;*   Executives work on diverse platforms.

Pocket-sized = *small;*   He is only a pocket-sized cricketer.

Put to sword = *diminish, destroy;*   They put the bowling attack to sword.

Keep one's poise = *remain calm;*   My mother keeps her poise in difficult times.

Prop up one's coffer = *get more money, profit;* Jude's only aim is to prop up her coffers.

Unput down quality = *unending, permanent;* The book has unput down quality.

Take a potshot = *criticise, hit out;* He took a potshot at Martha.

One-trick pony = *depend on one man;* A business house requires competent staff, not one-trick pony.

Have porcupine power = *many sided;* HRD managers have porcupine powers.

Pry into = *look stealthily;* The boy is prying into my personal life.

Pencil in = *schedule, to take place;* The conference is pencilled in for March.

A phone-call away = *very near;* Our salesman is only a phone-call away from you.

Reach a high point = *reach the top;* He has reached a high point of his career.

A pot-boiler = *cater to public taste;* The movie is a family pot-boiler.

Push for = *try to achieve;* States are pushing for more autonomy.

Talking point = *focus of attention;* He has become a talking point.

Rich pool of talents = *on large scale;* The company has a rich pool of talents.

Pyrrhic victory = *won at great cost;* Allied forces won a pyrrhic victory against Germany.

Make one's point = *put across views;* I made my point but he failed to listen to it.

Point-blank = *bluntly;* They rejected the offer point-blank.

Point of honour = *action affecting conscience;* I refused to talk to Mike as a point of honour.

Have a pop at something = *attack;* He had a pop at his opponents.

Postcard perfect = *like beautiful photograph;* I saw postcard perfect cottages in the valley.

Straight out of a picture = *as attractive as a picture;* The castle is straight out of a picture.

Prime position = *important place;* He is holding a prime position in the organisation.

Pride oneself on = *be proud of;* Keith will pride himself on his knowledge.

At present = *now;* I can't help you at present.

Pet and perky = *attractive;* Viola is a pert and perky girl.

In a quagmire = *in awkward position;* Jane is in a quagmire.

Quail at = *feel fear;* They quailed at the sight of a tiger.

Quake in one's boots = *tremble with fear;* When the firing started we quaked in our boots.

Give quality assurance = *assurance about quality;* The salesman gave me quality assurance about the refrigerator.

In a quandary = *uncertain, undecided;* She has put me in a quandary.

Quantum jump = *abrupt change;* There is a quantum jump in prices.

Give no quarter = *show no mercy;* The army gave no quarter to enemy.

A queer card = *strange person;* He always remained a queer card.

In queer street = *in debt;* He is in queer street.

Queer the pitch = *destroy, spoil;* The work is going on well but he will queer the pitch.

A query = *a question;* Can you solve this query?

A question of time = *to happen soon;*   I will leave the job. It is a question of time.

Field the question = *face;*   The minister fielded some questions in parliament.

Come into question = *come for discussion;*   This issue came into question during the meeting.

Quick on the update = *understand well;*   The boy is quick on the update.

Out of question = *unlikely to be discussed;*   Tony's demand is out of question.

In queue = *to be discussed;*   Many questions are in queue.

Quick-fix solution = *speedy but insufficient;*   There is no quick-fix solution to the problem.

The quintessence of something = *intrinsic part;*   Good technique is the quintessence of batting.

Breathtaking quality = *fantastic, fabulous;*   The product has breathtaking quality.

Something quixotic = *foolish, unrealistic;*   The scheme is absolutely quixotic.

One's rabbit = *prey;*   A poor batsman is a good bowler's rabbit.

Race through = *move, pass swiftly;*   Many ideas raced through my mind.

In the race = *compete for success;*   The post is vacant and Collins is also in the race.

Race against time = *do fast;*   You are racing against time.

On the rack = *feel distressed;*   Bill is on the rack.

Rack up = *achieve;*   The company is racking up a huge profit.

In the racket = *one's business;*   Joy is in publicity racket.

A racketeer = *dishonest, deceitful;*   He is a racketeer.

Racy style = *thrilling, entertaining;*   Write in racy style much like Dickens.

The rage = *in fashion;*   Cybercafes are the rage of this age.

Beside with rage = *violent anger;*   Tom is beside with rage.

Go off the rails = *behave violently;*   Nora has gone off the rails.

On the rails = *work in normal way;*   The industry is back on the rails.

A rainbow coalition = *a formation of different parties;* There are rainbow coalitions in many countries.

Raise eyebrows = *show surprise;* The move has raised many eyebrows.

Raise the roof = *make great noise;* The children in the class raised the roof.

Ramp up = *increase the output;* The producers have ramped up the production.

On the rampage = *a violent crowd, group;* The robbers are on the rampage.

At random = *without notice, decision;* The passengers were checked at random.

Close ranks = *become united;* All parties close ranks during war.

From the ranks = *progress because of one's efforts;* The manager is from the ranks.

At any rate = *in every way;* She will stand by me at any rate.

Rat on someone = *disclose secrets;* Andrew is a noble man. He will not rat on you.

Rat race = *compete with others to get power;* I will not join this rat race.

Rattle sabres = *get aggressive;* The enemy country is rattling sabres.

Win raves = *receive praise;* The movie is winning raves from all people.

Razor-sharp = *very sharp;* He has razor-sharp memory.

Read between the lines = *know the hidden meaning;* Though your statement is ambiguous, I can read between the lines.

At the reading = *available for use;* Keep your gun at the ready in the forest.

Ready-made = *available without preparation;* They eat ready-made food.

Realpolitik = *based on realism;* We believe in realpolitik.

Reap the harvest = *bear the consequences;* We reap the harvest of our misdeeds.

Bring the rear = *at the end;* All went down the road and Kim brought up the rear.

Rearguard action = *a defensive move;* The full-back staged a rearguard action and saved the team.

To be reckoned with = *a thing not to be ignored;* South-Asian countries have become a force to be reckoned with.

Set the record straight = *present correct version;* The letter contained mistakes. Now we should set the record straight.

In reduced circumstances = *poor state;* After retirement, Geff is living in reduced circumstances.

Red zone = *dangerous area;* Don't go to that red zone.

Frosty relation = *cold, unfriendly;* These two countries have frosty relations.

A broken reed = *ineffective, weak person;* After his wife's death, he is a broken reed.

Rev up = *boost up, increase;* The policy will rev up economy.

Rare to go = *keen, ready;*   The team is raring up to play and win.

As regards = *regarding, concerning;*   As regards economy, the government policy is clear.

With regard to = *regarding, about;*   Mike asked me with regard to your conduct.

Reigning champion = *holding title;*   Tyson is a reigning world champion.

Give free rein = *full freedom of action;*   Don was given full rein to chart out his plan.

Keep a tight rein = *to allow little freedom;*   His mother keeps a tight rein on his activities.

In relative = *compared with;*   Paul is doing better relative to Peter.

Relieve feelings = *use harsh words when angry;*   Tim relieved feelings upon seeing his opponent.

Curtain raiser = *a preceding thing;*   What you see is only a curtain raiser.

Remiss about = *careless;*   The police was remiss about security measures.

Renaissance man = *talented person;*   The professor is a Renaissance man.

A renegade = *unfaithful person;*   Heath is a renegade politician.

Renounce the world = *a recluse, spiritual man;*   Titus has renounced the world.

Repartee = *witty, quick remark;*   Oscar Wilde was known for his brilliant repartees.

A reservoir of something = *source, place;* Ireland has been a reservoir of literary figures.

In the last resort = *finally;* In the last resort we will have to go.

Rest on one's shoulder = *depend;* The responsibility rests on your shoulder.

Rest on = *depend, trust;* Mani rested all her hopes on me.

Without result = *without gain, profit;* He worked hard without result.

Revolve around = *essential point;* Monica's life revolves around her husband.

Real doll = *attractive girl;* Agnes is a real doll.

Take for a ride = *cheat, deceive;* Don't take this innocent boy for a ride.

Without rhyme and reason = *without solid reason;* Tobby's statement has no rhyme and reason.

Tear to ribbons = *damage badly;* The entire system has been torn to ribbons.

To rid of = *make free;* Let us rid the world of terrorism.

Get rid of = *to be free from bad thing;* You should get rid of this bad habit.

A riddle = *a puzzle;* Life after dealth is a riddle.

Talk in riddles = *talk in an ambiguous way;* Wright talks in riddles.

Ride for a fall = *resulting in defeat;* An arrogant person rides for a fall.

A rough ride = *bad time;* The workers gave a rough ride to the manager.

Ride out = *pass safely;*   The management has ridden out the strike.

Run rife = *go unchecked, common;*   Rumour is running rife that the prices of key shares will fall.

Rifle through = *search through;*   The thief rifled through the room and took away all the gold.

Riff-raff = *disrespectable person;*   Dickens wrote about the riff-raffs of human society.

In the right = *justified in action;*   A priest is generally in the right.

In right mind = *sane, sensible;*   The judge is in right mind.

Relaxed atmosphere = *friendly and peaceful;*   Talks were held in a relaxed atmosphere.

Ride high = *high expectation, chance;*   Hope is riding high that peace will prevail.

Set things to rights = *bring to correct state;*   Things are in bad shape. You set them to rights.

Right-hand man = *dependable, a confidant;*   He is the prime minister's right-hand man.

Ringside view = *complete, up to date;*   Give me a ringside view of the situation.

Ripple effect = *wide, far reaching;*   War has a ripple effect on society.

Rip-roaring = *boistrous, vigorous;*   It is a rip-roaring comedy.

A rising star = *promising, bright;*   He is a rising star of Indian cricket.

Risky job = *dangerous work;*   To diffuse this crisis is a risky job.

Ritzy and glitzy = *stylish, glamorous;* It is a ritzy and glitzy hotel.

Reach the dead end = *an end of something;* Neil has reached the dead end of his career.

Hit the roadblock = *come to a stop;* The project suddenly hit the roadblock.

Rocky road = *a difficult thing;* To get success in life is a rocky road.

Rough up = *beat badly;* The robbers roughed me up.

A roaring success = *very successful;* The play was a roaring success.

A roaring trade = *very profitable;* He is doing a roaring trade.

Rock the boat = *cause trouble, danger;* Don't rock the boat of the country's economy.

Rocketing speed = *very fast;* The ball went past the fielder with rocketing speed.

Rule with an iron rod = *rule strictly, sternly;* Hitler ruled with an iron rod.

On the rocks = *in difficulty;* Their marriage is on the rocks.

Rock-bottom = *at the lowest level;* The share market is at rock-bottom.

Role model = *an exemplary person;* Indira Gandhi was a role model for many people.

On a roll = *having a long success;* The company is on a roll.

Roll out = *bring out, launch;* Japan is rolling out a new car.

Roller coaster = *pass through changes;* The West Indies victory in the ODI was a roller coaster.

Rollicking humour = *lively, jovial;* The book is full of rollicking humour.

Give no room = *chance;* A good management gives no room to incompetent workers.

Make room for = *give space, way;* Make room for the servant to clear it.

Root cause = *main reason;* It is the root cause of the problem.

Strike at the roots = *destroy the main part;* Poverty is striking at the roots of our society.

Root out = *destroy, remove;* The government should root out corruption.

On the ropes = *facing defeat;* The team is on the ropes.

Learn the ropes = *learn tricks;* A new worker should learn the ropes from senior workers.

A rough time = *hard, difficult, bad;* The boss gave him a hard time because his work was bad.

Round the corner = *very close, near;* Your examinations are round the corner.

Rub shoulders = *mix, get familiar;* Gracy rubs shoulders with teachers.

Cross the Rubicon = *never to return;* He has crossed the Rubicon and joined robbers.

Make it a rule = *make a habit;* Make it a rule not to come late.

Rule the roost = *in total control;* Only moneyed people are ruling the roost.

On the run = *try to escape;* The thief is on the run.

Run against = *chance to meet;* Yesterday, I ran against my very old friend.

Run down = *hit, criticise;* Don't run him down.

Run out = *face shortage;* We are running out of ration.

Rough-house = *fight, create violence;* The bullies rough-house on the street.

Roil the image = *spoil;* They roil the image of the country.

Run hard = *work hard;* John is running hard for Democratic nomination.

Unveil a report = *open, make public;* The minister unveiled a report on the country's economy.

Redemption road = *road to recovery;* Brian Lara is on redemption road and scored a century.

Roll into one = *combined in one person;* He is a teacher, writer and thinker-all rolled into one.

Riot of colours = *varied display;* The stage was a riot of colours.

Run into trouble = *face, in for;* My friend is running into trouble.

Doing the round = *pass from man to man;* This story is doing the round that he is dead.

See red = *get angry;* The high prices will make the consumers see red.

A revelation = *a surprising thing;* Zidane was a revelation in Germany.

Rock-star days = *days of rock-star music;*   We remember those rock-star days.

Raft of rules = *many, a large number;*   The country issued a raft of rules.

Rise to bait = *accept an enticing thing;*   She refused to rise to his bait.

Create with rose water = *easily;*   Revolutions are not created with rose water.

Rise from ashes = *rise from destruction;*   The Austrialian cricket team can rise from the ashes.

Romp home = *an easy winner;*   Manchester United romped home to victory.

Ride high = *become successful;*   The economy of Japan is riding high.

On the road to recovery = *recover after early loss;*   The country is on the road to recovery after war.

S

Get the sack = *dismiss from job;* The boss sacked Joy.

Sabotage something = *damage, harm;* The opposition party sabotaged the plan.

To be saddled with = *have responsibility;* Greg is saddled with money problem.

In the saddle = *in complete control;* Our party is in the saddle.

In safe hands = *protected from harm;* George is in safe hands of his teacher.

On the safe side = *not to take risk;* We should bat first to be on the safe side.

A safe bet = *dependable thing;* Invest money in this company. It is a safe bet.

Saga of sorrow = *a sad story;* The old man told me his saga of sorrow.

Sail on = *move smoothly;* The organisation is sailing on smoothly.

Salad days = *days of youth;* In old age we remember our salad days.

Up for sale = *for purchase;* The books are for sale.

On sale = *offer for buying;*   Many items are on sale.

Salutary effects = *good results;*   The scheme will have salutary effects on the public.

Give sanctuary to = *freedom from arrest;*   Some countries give sanctuary to terrorists.

Happy as a sandboy = *very happy;*   Stan is as happy as a sandboy.

Sandwiched between = *squeezed between two;*   Pet was sandwiched between Jack and Jill.

Run into the sand = *come to a stop;*   The economic drive ran into the sand.

Packed like sardines = *a crowded place;*   In the small room we were packed like sardines.

Satellite town = *nearly, adjacent;*   Gurgaon is a satellite town of Delhi.

To one's satisfaction = *to one's liking, desire;*   We played to our satisfaction.

Save the situation = *a solution to a difficulty;*   There were riots but the police saved the situation.

Business savvy = *Shrewd in business;*   The Japanese are business savvy.

Come under the scanner = *under scrutiny;*   His activities have come under police scanner.

The scheme of things = *in system;*   Bill's plan and ideas are not in the scheme of things.

Scissor out = *remove, cut;*   The panel scissored out this portion from the movie.

Scott-free = *without getting punishment;*   Some criminals got off scot-free.

Scrape through = *pass;* Hall scraped through the examination.

Scrape acquaintance with = *develop;* DeCosta scraped acquaintance with Suzy.

Scratch for = *find out, search;* They are scratching around for a teacher.

From scratch = *from the beginning;* Smith started his business from scratch.

Put the screws = *put pressure;* Put the screws on an errant child.

Screw up = *use, bring up;* You should screw up all your resources and succeed.

Screw-up = *in a mess, disorder;* The whole system is a screw-up.

Have no scruple = *have no hesitation;* Dodger has no scruple about cheating people.

At sea = *unable to understand;* De Monte was speaking French and I was completely at sea.

Sea change = *great change;* There is a sea change in the economic policy of the country.

Seal off = *close;* They have sealed off the border.

Set seal on = *give approval;* The government has set seal on the new project.

Burst at the seams = *overcrowded, full of;* The room was bursting at the seams with children.

Second to none = *incomparable, best;* Shakespeare's works are second to none.

Second thoughts = *after reconsideration;*   On second thoughts I found this product very good.

Make no secret of = *make clear;*   Steve made no secret of this work.

See over = *inspect, examine;*   I shall see over the property before I purchase it.

Seedy character = *bad, dishonest;*   Darwin is a seedy character.

Seethe with rage = *very angry;*   He was fuming and seething with rage.

In sequence = *in order;*   Arrange the numbers in sequence.

Set off = *start, cause;*   These strong steps will set off a strong public reaction.

Set out = *begin, start;*   We have set out to achieve our target.

Set up something = *begin as occupation;*   Dr.Smith has set up his practice in Allahabad.

Sever ties = *break relationship;*   The two countries have severed their ties.

No shadow of doubt = *very clear;*   There is no shadow of doubt about his honesty.

Shady dealings = *dishonest, deceitful;*   He is a man of shady dealings.

Shake off = *remove, get rid of;*   Sometimes it is difficult to shake off the past memories.

Shaky foundation = *weak, fallible;*   These students have shaky foundations.

Shake-up = *drastic change;*   The political system requires a shake-up.

In a shambles = *in bad shape, disorder;*   The company is in a shambles.

Shangri-La = *a place like paradise;*   This beautiful valley is like Shangri-La.

Get into shape = *make better, stronger;*   He is trying to get the team into shape.

Out of shape = *without usual shape;*   The picture is out of shape.

The shape of things to come = *show the future of things;*   The strong statement is the shape of things to come.

A shark = *dishonest person, money grabber;*   There are many sharks around.

Sharpen up = *hone up, improve;*   Little Dick is sharpening his memory.

Sheet anchor = *responsible person;*   Fleming is the sheet anchor of New Zealand batting.

Shell-shock = *disturbed, perturbed;*   The children were shell-shocked to hear the bad news of their father.

A good shepherd = *leader;*   Our teacher is a good shepherd.

Shift ground = *say or do the opposite;*   Politicians often shift their ground.

Take the shine off = *destroy, spoil;*   Your bad actions have taken the shine off your good family.

Shining star = *promising, brilliant person;*   He is a shining star in the world of football.

Go short = *lack, not have enough;*   We are going short of food.

In short = *in a nutshell, in brief;*   He is a Gandhian in short.

Make short work of = *defeat, destroy;* Allied forces made short work of German tanks.

No short cut = *no other way;* There is no short cut to success except hard work.

Give short shrift = *reject, dismiss;* They gave short shrift to my plan and policy.

Something short-sighted = *narrow, limited;* These views and ideas are short-sighted.

On the same wavelength = *equal, of same type;* Jim and I are on the same wavelength.

Look over the shoulder = *worried, insecure;* There is a crisis in the market and traders are looking over their shoulders.

Shove off = *get lost, go away;* Please shove off from here.

Show one's face = *appear;* The director showed his face at the last moment.

Show teeth = *show agression, power;* Drug traffickers show their teeth to the government.

Show off = *display to others;* The model shows off her shapely legs.

A showdown = *fracas, fight, confrontation;* There was a showdown between the Democratic and Labour party.

A showpiece = *an exemplary thing;* The new car is a showpiece of Japanese technology.

Give the shudders = *create fear;* The idea of ghosts gives me the shudders at night.

Shut up shop = *stop, cease work;* The player is weak and old. He should shut up shop.

Shuttle diplomacy = *hold talks with reluctant parties;* Kissinger was known for shuttle diplomacy.

Have a shy at = *hit at something;* The fielder had a shy at the stumps.

A Shylock = *money grabber;* He is a Shylock.

Sick and tired of = *fed up;* The teacher is sick and tired of Graham's lame excuses.

Side with = *give help, support;* A mother sides with her children.

By the side of = *near, close to;* My shop is by the side of a hotel.

On one's side = *to one's benefit, advantage;* Everything is on our side.

Take sides = *support one against another;* Simpson will not take sides in this dispute.

Sideline something = *remove, ignore;* The boy has been sidelined from the team.

Side-splitting = *very humorous, lively;* He told me a side-splitting anecdote.

Sieve through = *examine thoroughly;* The manager sieves through the report.

Lose sight of = *unable to see, ignore;* You can never lose sight of his good quality.

On sight = *when seen;* The police will arrest him on sight.

Set sight on = *desire to get, achieve;* Brazil has set sight on the World Cup.

Sign of the times = *show prevailing situation;* Mayhem and murders are the signs of the times.

Sign up = *engage on contract, employment;* The company has signed up the actor for advertisement.

Silky soft = *smooth, fine;* She has silky soft skin.

Single-minded = *have one purpose;* Croft has pursued his studies with single-minded purpose of getting success in life.

Sink differences = *drop, forget;* We should sink our differences.

A sinking ship = *failing organisation;* The company is a sinking ship.

Sink or swim = *fail or succeed at one's risk;* I don't know whether Shaw will sink or swim.

See-saw = *up and down, various changes;* Dorina has passed through many see-saws of life.

Sit tight = *remain firm, nor to take chance;* Let us sit tight and not do anything silly.

A sitting duck = *unprotected person;* A poor person is always a sitting duck.

Hit for a six = *rebuff, overcome;* Heath talked nonsense and I hit him for a six.

Size up something = *know, perceive;* A leopard sizes up the situation very early.

Skate on thin ice = *take dangerous course;* Ruth is skating on thin ice and will fail.

Skeletons in the cupboard = *dirty secrets;* There are many skeletons in some politician's cupboard.

By the skin of teeth = *within narrow limits;* He is playing by the skin of his teeth.

Skip something = *give up, leave;*   If you don't like it, skip it.

To skylark = *play jokes, pass time;*   He is skylarking with a child.

Slack off = *decrease, reduce;*   The sea tide has slacked off.

On the song = *very happy;*   Lee has taken five wickets and is on the song.

For a song = *very cheaply;*   He sold the girl for a song.

Slap on the face = *insult, affront;*   What Kimi said is a slap on my face.

Slated for = *due, schedule;*   The talks are slated for December.

Sleep on something = *delay, ignore;*   The clerk is sleeping on the files.

Up one's sleeve = *secret ideas, plans;*   I have something up my sleeve.

Give the slip = *avoid, escape, run away;*   The thief gave the policeman the slip.

On a slippery slope = *wrong course;*   He is on a slippery slope.

Slog out = *play, fight with aggression;*   The batsmen will slog out in the last overs.

Small potatoes = *very small;*   His work was small potatoes.

Go to smash = *get destroyed, ruined;*   The entire plan went to smash.

A smashing success = *great, excellent;*   The movie is a smashing success.

Smell a rat = *something dubious;* I smell a rat in his dealings.

Go up in smoke = *achieve nothing;* Ivan's efforts went up in smoke.

A smokescreen = *a device to hide reality;* The new peace plan is a smokescreen to hide public anger.

A smooth sailing = *easy, not difficult;* The examination was a smooth sailing for Miki.

Snake in the grass = *danger, deceitful person;* Be careful of Phil, he is a snake in the grass.

One's socks off = *do with interest, fervour;* They play with their socks off.

Have soft corner for = *love, affection;* Camila has a soft corner for Keith.

As solid as a rock = *firm, strong;* Gilchrist is as solid as a rock behind the stumps.

Sore point = *a distressing issue;* They reached a sore point in their discussion.

To soup up = *make more attractive;* We use advertisements to soup up our products.

Go sour = *go bad, unpleasant;* Their relationship has gone sour.

Seeds of sorrow = *thing which gives bad results;* He is sowing the seeds of sorrow for the family.

Spark trouble = *create, start;* The issue will spark trouble in the public.

Make a spectacle of oneself = *draw attention in a ridiculous way;* She danced in such a way that she made a spectacle of herself.

Spell out = *explain;* The manager will spell out the whole issue.

Speedy remedy = *quick, early;* The problem requires speedy remedy.

In a snap = *quickly, in no time;* He will bring the food in a snap.

Spike guns = *prevent a plan;* Ashly wanted to harm our business but we spiked his guns.

Spill the beans = *disclose secrets;* She accidentally spilled the beans about the murder.

Spine-chilling = *creating terror and excitement;* His encounter with the tiger was spine-chilling.

Money-spinning = *produce, give money;* This product is a money-spinning proposition.

In a spot = *face difficulty;* Eva is in a spot.

On the spot = *soon, without delay;* The children will write it on the spot.

Spot advertisement = *a television ad;* We see many spot advertisements during the serials.

Spread like wildfire = *spread quickly;* The news of his arrival spread like wildfire.

On a spree = *act with unlimited freedom;* Neil has gone on a shopping spree.

On the spur of the moment = *without prethought;* Viola left the room on the spur of the moment.

Spy on = *watch, observe;* He is spying on his wife.

A square deal = *fair treatment;* The master gives square deal to his servant.

Back to square one = *return to starting point;* Sorry, our busines is back to square one.

Hold the stage = *exercise control, in command;* Burke holds the stage in the party.

To stage = *comeback;* He staged a dramatic comeback in cricket.

Set the stage = *prepare background;* He set the stage for economic reforms.

Set stake = *in danger, at risk;* My career is at stake.

Stall one's move = *stop, obstruct;* The opposition party stalled the move of the government.

Stand a chance = *scope, opportunity;* Brown stands a chance to get the job.

Stand rock-solid = *remain firm, resolute;* Bradman stood rock-solid against all bowling attacks.

Stand-off = *a deadlock between two parties;* There is stand-off between the US and Iran.

Star-struck = *in wonder, impressed;* I was star-struck to see his brilliant performance.

Star-studded = *filled with famous actors, player;* The football team of Brazil is star-studded.

A doubtful starter = *uncertain to participate;* Johnson is a doubtful starter for the Test match.

Startling quality = *fantastic, excellent;* Though the writer is young, he has startling qualities.

Be starved of = *short of, lack;* The company is starved of capital.

Stave off = *avoid, avert;* Only serious peace efforts can stave off war.

Steal a march = *get advantage over others;* A good businessman steals a march on his rivals.

Get steamed up = *get angry;* Evans gets steamed up at the slightest provocation.

Steam in = *ready to join competition;* Johnson is steaming in and will join the US team.

Run out of steam = *lose initiative and interest;* The Indian team is running out of steam.

Steely edge = *resolute, hard, tough;* There is a steely edge to his writing.

Stem the root = *remove;* Let us stem the root of corruption.

Steady the nerves = *keep normal, calm;* His brilliant innings will steady the nerves of the team.

Mind step = *behave, act carefully;* Mind your step before you enter a business.

On sticky wicket = *uncomfortable position;* New laws will put traders on sticky wickets.

Stick with = *continue with;* We will stick with the same policy.

Take stock = *assess, know, review;* Take stock of the situation before we make a decision.

To stonewall something = *block, delay;* The Labour party stonewalled all the moves of Conservative party.

Stony-hearted = *ruthless, cruel;* A stony-hearted man.

Put a stop to = *end something;* I put a stop to his antics.

A storm in a teacup = *anger about small matter;* His annoyance was a storm in a teacup.

Get something straight = *make something clear;* Dear friend, you should get the matter straight.

Strain every nerve = *make great effort;* Paul is straining every nerve to scale the peak.

On stream = *available;* Many new motorcycles are on stream.

Streets ahead = *far better;* Our college is streets ahead of other colleges.

Go from strength to strength = *get increasing success;* Manchester United went from strength to strength and won the championship.

Stroke of luck = *fortunately;* It was a stroke of luck that I saw my old friend.

Go strong = *remain energetic;* Though he is seventy years old, he is still going strong.

Strong on = *competent, good at;* He is strong on acting.

Be stumped = *confused, difficult thing;* I was stumped by his remark.

In quick succession = *one after another;* All these events happened in quick succession.

Suck dry = *finish a person's resources;* Anne sucked her mother dry.

Under the sun = *in the world, on earth;* There is nothing new under the sun.

Sunny side = *pleasant side;* Ray looks at the sunny side of a thing.

In support of = *show support;* They staged a demonstration in support of the government.

For sure = *without any doubt;* You take it for sure that Colins will play.

Look spruce and sprightly = *lively, attractive;* Beatrice looks spruce and sprightly in this dress.

Something swanky = *very stylish and luxurious;* Executives stay in swanky hotels.

Swansong = *last performance, public appearance;* Last World Cup was Roberto Carlos' swansong.

Swashbuckling = *daring, flamboyant;* Keith Miller of Australia was a swashbuckling cricketer.

Make sweeping changes = *bring about great changes;* He made sweeping changes in management.

Swim with the tide = *according to;* Most of the people swim with the tide of time.

Get into the swing of things = *get familiar;* The new employee will get into the swing soon.

Face a shutdown = *rejection, removal;* The minister is facing a shutdown from power.

Reach full stretch = *get maximum, reach top;* He has reached full stretch of his talents.

Sure-fire remedy = *certain;* Economic growth is a sure-fire remedy for a country's development.

Strap for = *short of, lack;* We are strapped for cash.

In sync with = *in agreement;* The US is in sync with Russia on the nuclear deal.

Stay true = *faithful, sincere;* People should stay true to their country.

Stay tight-lipped = *silent;* The media stayed tight-lipped about the news.

Send strong signal = *serious, important message;*   There is a strong signal that he will not resign from leadership.

Stick to side = *support, back up;*   He sticks to our side.

Spawn a new line = *start, begin;*   She spawned a new line in fashion industry.

Slam the report = *hit, criticise;*   He slammed all reports about his failure.

Spit fire = *express anger;*   Robin is spitting fire.

Stay clear = *remain away, free;*   We should stay clear of this controversy.

Change stripes = *habit, behaviour;*   The terrorist organisations should change stripes.

Spit-shined = *shining;*   The model wears spit-shined shoes.

Cast a spotlight = *focus, show importance;*   The book casts a spotlight on environment.

Send shockwaves = *create disturbed feelings;*   The event sent shockwaves across the country.

Storm front of something = *favourite;*   Austria is the storm front of the tournament.

Shoot in the foot = *commit silly mistakes;*   He is playing wrong shots and shooting himself in the foot.

Sidetrack the issue = *distract, avoid;*   It was an important issue but he sidetracked it.

T

Keep tab on = *watch, observe;*   Keep a tab on his activities.

On the table = *An offer to be discussed;*   My plan is on the table.

Turn the tables = *reverse the situation;*   The company turned the tables on its rivals.

With tails up = *in buoyant mood, confident;*   They are playing with their tails up.

Tailor-made = *suiting a situation;*   He made a tailor-made statement to please all.

A tailpiece = *the end part;*   The tailpiece of a story should be convincing.

Send into a tailspin = *panic, chaos;*   The fall in share prices sent traders into a tailspin.

Tail off = *decrease, diminish;*   The impact of the policy is tailing off.

Take off = *succeed, popular;*   The new policy will not take off at all.

Taker = *person who accepts;*   There are no takers for this job.

Talismanic figure = *powerful and good;* The new coach is a talismanic figure.

A tall order = *unacceptable demand;* The salary you demand is a tall order.

To tame = *control, check;* The government should tame the price rise.

A tangled web = *a complicated situation;* Ben found himself in a tangled web.

On target = *hit the object;* He was bang on target and scored a fantastic goal.

Take a person to task = *criticise, scold;* The principal took the teacher to task.

In tatters = *in shambles, ruined;* The peace agreement is in tatters now.

Teach a lesson = *set someone right;* I taught him the lesson of his life.

Telegenic face = *appealing on TV;* She has a telegenic face.

Telling effect = *significant, good;* These steps will have telling effect on public.

A tempting offer = *attractive, appealing;* Steve refused that tempting offer.

Tension-packed = *tense, uncomfortable;* It was a tension-packed atmosphere.

On tenterhooks = *in suspence, doubt;* Speak clearly and don't keep me on tenterhooks.

Come to terms with = *accept, reconcile to;* Ben has come to terms with many problems.

Put to the test = *know effectiveness;* The board put the candidate to the test.

Stand the test of time = *remain good;* The car will stand the test of time.

Testing ground = *an area to test something;* The poor are the testing ground of mankind.

Textbook style = *perfectly, nicely;* He plays in a textbook style.

A thaw in relations = *flexibility, warmness;* There is a thaw in US-German relations.

Thick with = *very close, friendly;* Sheila is thick with Sam.

In the thick of = *busy with something;* Laker is in the thick of the matter.

Through thick and thin = *in every way;* I am with you through thick and thin.

Have a thin time = *bad, uncomfortable;* Jane and James are having a thin time.

A thing of the past = *which no longer exists;* What you describe is a thing of the past.

A thing or two = *some useful things;* Corbett told me a thing or two about nature.

Think out = *consider in detail;* We are thinking out a new scheme for the poor.

Think over = *think carefully;* You should think over the entire issue.

Thirsty for = *keen to know;* The lawyer is thirsty for details of the case.

Thrash out = *discuss sincerely;*   Let us thrash out our differences.

Hang by a thread = *in delicate condition;*   His life hangs by a thread.

Thrills and spills = *dangerous excitements;*   Grand Prix race has its own thrills and spills.

At each other's throats = *fight persistently;*   These two boys are always at each other's throats.

Through and through = *completely;*   Cain is a rogue through and through.

Throw in the towel = *accept defeat;*   Ray has thrown in the towel and is out of the championship.

Throw on = *attach something;*   The army threw itself on the enemy.

Throwaway prices = *very cheap;*   I purchased a shirt on throwaway prices.

Thumb nose at = *show contempt;*   We thumb our nose at our enemy.

Thumbs down = *disapproval;*   The company got the thumbs down from Japan to build the car.

Tick off = *scold, rebuke;*   His wife ticked him off.

Ticket out of = *a way out;*   Hard work is a ticket out of poverty.

To ticket a person = *impose fine, challan;*   If you don't follow traffic rules, the police will ticket you.

In a tight spot = *in difficulty;*   After the death of her husband, Liza finds herself in a tight spot.

The time of one's life = *time of exceeding joy;* On the beaches of West Indies I had the time of my life.

Time-consuming = *take a very long time;* Though the project is good, it is time-consuming.

Time off = *recreation time from work;* A little time off increases efficiency.

Take time out = *a little break from play;* The basket ball players take a time out from their game.

Time-tested = *reliable, permanent;* It is a time-tested formula.

Time-server = *change with situation;* Most of the people are selfish and time-servers.

Tip the scale = *a deciding force, factor;* During the interview Bob tipped the scale in my favour.

Tip off = *pass the information;* She tipped off the police about his whereabouts.

In tip-top = *in fine shape;* My car is still in tip-top condition.

Something titanic = *powerful, great;* The Greeks fought many titanic battles.

Toe the line = *follow someone's policy;* Prakash is toeing the line of the Congress party.

Tone up = *strengthen;* This medicine will tone up your body.

Tune down = *make the noise less harsh;* Please tune down your transistor.

Give tongue = *speak freely, express feelings;* Give tongue to your ideas.

Shrill-tongued = *harsh sound, voice;* Noreen is a shrill-tongued woman.

Armed to the teeth = *completely equipped with arms;* The robbers were armed to the teeth.

In the teeth of = *in the face of fierce attack;* The operation was carried out in the teeth of enemy attack.

Teething troubles = *early temporary problems;* Every project has some teething problems.

Toothless tiger = *powerless person, thing;* That country is no more a toothless tiger.

On top of the world = *very happy;* After winning the World Cup the Australian team was on top of the world.

On top of the tree = *reach the highest point;* Bill Gates is on top of the tree.

Something top-notch = *of high quality;* It is a top-notch sea resort.

Torch-bearer = *a leading thing, person;* We are torch-bearers in the field of electronics.

A torrent of criticism = *violent and sudden;* The government faced a torrent of criticism from the opposition.

Torrid time = *difficult period;* It was a torrid time of my life.

Tottering economy = *weak, unsteady;* The country is having a tottering economy.

In touch with = *familiar, uptodate;* Keep in touch with new developments.

Out of touch = *unfamiliar, not knowing;* I am absolutely out of touch with these ideas.

Touch-me-not gesture = *not to come close;* Agnes made a touch-me-not gesture, and the boy went away.

Rough and tough = *solid, strong;*   These tracking shoes are rough and tough.

Talk through one's hat = *foolishly;*   Robin always talks through his hat.

Tide over = *over come a difficulty;*   I will tide over the problem.

Lose track of = *lose touch, remain uninformed;*   I lost track of Rosy.

Off the track = *depart from right line;*   On this point Linda is off the track.

On track = *on the right course;*   Sibil is on track and will succeed.

Track down = *find out, search out;*   The police will track him down soon.

Track record = *past performance;*   Joy's track record is not good.

Trade off = *exchange for profit;*   Some countries trade off economic gains to get more political clout.

Toy with an idea = *consider without seriousness;*   It is an important idea. Don't toy with it.

Have trademarks = *standard, qualities;*   Lucy has all the trademarks of a politician.

Trade charges = *exchange;*   They are are trading charges against one another.

A trafficker = *deal in illegal things;*   Tim is a drug trafficker.

In train = *come up, progress;*   New inventions and discoveries are in train.

Train of thought = *a line of thinking;*   Sindi could not know my train of thought.

Translate into reality = *change into;* Good policies should be translated into reality.

Have the trappings = *qualities, features;* Rose has all the trappings of a cricketer.

Treasure trove = *a store of valuable things;* Jungle Tales is a treasure trove of wildlife.

Out of one's tree = *foolish, stupid;* Ken is now out of his tree.

Trendy trend = *direction of fashion world;* Young boys and girls follow the trendy trends.

On trial = *being tested, examined;* The new drug is on trial.

Pay tribute = *show respect;* We pay tribute to Isaac Newton.

Trick into = *deceive someone to do something;* Gill tricked him into stealing this book.

Trick out of = *deprive of money;* He tricked the old man out of his savings.

Do the trick = *get desired result;* I simply used a small nail and it did the trick.

Tricks of the trade = *special methods of a profession;* Soon Bill will know all tricks of the trade.

A trickle of something = *very small;* He gave me a trickle of money.

Tricky issue = *a difficult problem;* To solve the border issue is a tricky issue.

Trifle with = *treat lightly;* Don't trifle with Sophia.

Trigger-happy = *ready for violence;* They are trigger-happy terrorists.

Storm trooper = *who subdue opposition;* They are the storm troopers of our party.

On the trot = *one after another;* India lost easy chances on the trot.

Ask for trouble = *incur, invite problem;* If Julie goes alone at night, she will ask for trouble.

Troublemaker = *who causes problem;* This boy is a troublemaker.

Troubleshooter = *person who solves problem;* Call John. He is a troubleshooter.

Trouble spot = *a place of continuous violence;* Afghanistan is a trouble spot.

Play truant = *avoid going to school;* Chris plays truant, and will fail in the examination.

Have no truck with = *have no dealings;* Shane has no truck with this bad boy.

True to = *remain faithful to;* A good man is always true to his words.

True to life = *represent a thing correctly;* Dickens' description of Victorian society is true to life.

Come up trumps = *work better than expected;* Our team stood second and came up trumps.

In truth = *in reality;* Smith, in truth, is a vagabond.

Try hand at = *try to do for the first time;* Greg tried his hand at the new machine.

Trying time = *tough time;* I am passing through a trying time.

Go down the tube = *fail completely;* All his plans went down the tube.

Tuck away = *keep in secure place;* They tucked away their jewellery in the steel almirah.

Be tuned in = *know , aware of;* The government should be tuned in to the demand of the public.

Out of tune = *not in agreement;* Ricky's ideas are out of tune with the present age.

To the tune = *to the extent;* He received a loan to the tune of Rupees two crore.

Light at the end of the tunnel = *end of hardship;* Work hard and you will see light at the end of the tunnel.

One's turf = *personal area, territory;* Morris should not interfere with Nora's personal life. It is not his turf.

Turn one's back on = *ignore, leave;* I was in great trouble, but Arthur turned his back upon me.

Turn one's hand to = *try something different;* The engineer turned his hand to literature.

Turn over a new leaf = *become good and responsible;* He became a priest and turned over a new leaf in his life.

Turn to good account = *use as an advantage;* The situation was good and I turned it to good account.

Turn against = *become hostile;* Suddenly, Martin turned against me.

Turn down = *reject;* She turned down my offer.

Turn out = *prove to be;* The match turned out to be a drab affair.

Turnabout = *a complete and sudden change;* They made a turnabout in their policy.

Turnaround = *dramatic change with good results;* There is a turnaround in our profit.

Turn turtle = *a thing that turns upside down;* The bus turned turtle.

Under tutelage = *control, protection;* He is under the chairman's tutelage.

In a twinkling = *in no time, instantly;* My purse was stolen in a twinkling.

It takes two to tango = *both are responsible;* Rosa also fought with Mara. It takes two to tango.

Twists and turns = *ups and downs;* We all face many twists and turns in our life.

Tough line = *hard policy;* Let us take a tough line against the opposition.

Tread a cautious line = *act carefully;* The situation is bad. We should tread a cautious line.

Toe-turned ally = *unreliable partner;* We should not have any relation with a toe-turned ally.

Taboo and redline = *prohibition or refusal;* Terrorist group has no taboo and redline against any party.

Touch off = *start, begin;* It will touch off new controversy.

Tsunami-like proportion = *very dangerous;* AIDS is spreading with tsunami-like proportion.

Tough out = *face boldly;* We can tough out all challenges of life.

Full throttle = *full power, force;*   The country is in full throttle to get the contract.

On the table = *for discussion;*   Democracy is no more on the table in that country.

Test-tube = *thing to be examined;*   Kashmir is a test-tube for Indo-Pak relations.

In a tizzy = *nervous, agitated;*   The fall in economy sent the government in a tizzy.

Right trajectory = *right course, policy;*   We are on the right trajectory.

On one's tail = *behind, follow;*   The police is on a thief's tail.

Tally-ho = *excitement, keeness;*   There was a tally-ho about this new product.

To tower over someone = *surpass, superior;*   Scholari is a fine coach. He towers over all other coaches.

A testament = *a proof, fact;*   This new car is a testament of our firm's popularity.

A talkathon = *very long discussion;*   The Security Council had a talkathon on the peace plan.

A tinpot = *weak, poor;*   Blake is a tinpot leader.

There was no tomorrow = *without caring for result;*   He eats as if there is no tomorrow.

A tossup = *two equally good things;*   There is always a tossup between Cambridge and Oxford.

Ubiquitous = *present everywhere;*   Jeans are ubiquitous among young boys and girls.

Ugly duckling = *good beyond expectations;*   Glen solved all questions. He is an ugly duckling.

The ultimate = *the best thing of its kind;*   Sarah is the ultimate in beauty.

Issue an ultimatum = *give final notice;*   The authorities have issued an ultimatum to all shopkeepers to remove their shops from the area.

Ultra = *to the greatest degree;*   Karl is an ultra Communist.

Take umbrage at = *feel angry, annoyed;*   The public took umbrage at his statement.

Under the umbrella = *protection, influence;*   Some countries work under the UN umbrella.

Umbrella group = *small group under someone's protection;*   There are many umbrella groups of Al Qaida.

Umpteen times = *many, countless;*   I told you this umpteen times.

Unaccommodating nature = *unhelpful;*   Jason is a man of unaccommodating nature.

Unaccomplished task = *unfinished work;* Never leave any task unaccomplished.

Unaccountable money = *unjustifiable;* Nora has unaccountable money.

Unaccustomed to = *in unfamiliar, unusual way;* Pip and Pim went away in unaccustomed hurry.

Unacquainted with = *unfamiliar;* I am absolutely unacquainted with these surroundings.

Remain unaddressed = *unsolved, not considered;* The issue of poverty always remains unaddressed.

Unadulterated love = *pure;* Children give us unadulterated.

Remain unaffected = *show no effect;* A wise man remains unaffected by pleasure and power.

Unalloyed joy = *complete;* The beautiful valleys give you unalloyed joy.

Something unbelievable = *not to be believed;* Your story is unbelievable.

Unblemished = *faultless, undamaged;* Ron's character is unblemished.

Unaware of = *have no knowledge;* I am absolutely unaware of the situation.

Catch someone unawares = *without his knowledge;* The police caught him unawares.

Unbecoming of = *inappropriate;* It is unbecoming of you to abuse a child.

Unbothered about = *unconcerned;* Steve is unbothered about his father's illness.

Unbridgeable gap = *that can't be covered;* There is unbridgeable gap between the rich and the poor.

Unbridled freedom = *uncontrollable;* Mini wants unbridled freedom in her life.

Unburden one's heart = *relieve of sorrow and anxiety;* Tobby unburdened his heart to his uncle.

Uncanny feeling = *very strange, inexplicable;* Dora had an uncanny feeling that a pickpocket was coming after her.

Uncared for = *neglected;* Many old people remain uncared for in this world.

Unceremonious departure = *abrupt, lack dignity;* He made an unceremonious departure from the team.

Uncharted area = *uncovered, untouched;* The firm has covered many uncharted areas with success.

Clouds of uncertainty = *doubts;* The clouds of uncertainty hang over my future.

Unbutton someone = *make relax;* Don't feel shy. Please unbutton yourself.

Unclassified information = *not a secret, nonconfidential;* The spy has taken away unclassified information.

Uncle Sam = *US government;* Be careful, Uncle Sam is watching you.

Uncompromising attitude = *unwilling, unchanging;* The opposition party has adopted an uncompromising attitude.

Unconditional support = *without condition;* They have given unconditional support to the party.

Unconfirmed report = *without truth, validity;* This is an unconfirmed report.

Uncouth behaviour = *rough, lacking manners;* These boys are known for their uncouth behaviour.

Uncover the plot = *discover, open;* The secret agents uncovered a dangerous plot.

Undefined areas = *unclear, not defined;* There are still many undefined areas in the plan.

Under control = *under one's authority;* The little boy is under his father's control.

Under no circumstances = *in no way;* Under no circumstances can I help you.

Under one's obligation = *morally bound;* I am free. I am not under your obligation.

Under the thumb = *under control;* Rex is under the thumb of his wife.

Under duress = *threat, violence;* The kidnapped children are living under duress.

Under order = *act according to order;* We are under order to finish this job today.

Underhand dealing = *done in dishonest way;* Honest people don't like underhand dealings.

Under way = *in the progress, process;* Many new plans and policies are under way.

Under one's influence = *have an influence;* Wright is working under Bill's influence.

Under the illusion = *mistaken belief;* I was under the illusion that Dean would help me.

Work under someone = *below, control;* The teachers work under the principal.

Under the impression = *on the basis;* Justin is under the impression that Jill is his friend.

Undo the damage = *reverse the effect;* A timely help will undo the damage.

Undergo change = *experience;* Human society is undergoing many changes.

Go underground = *in hiding;* Many terrorists have gone underground.

Underdeveloped countries = *not fully advanced;* There are some underdeveloped countries in the world.

Under-resourced economy = *have insufficient resources;* Some poor countries have under-resourced economy.

Undermine something = *spoil, destroy;* One mistake can undermine your plan.

Sweep under the carpet = *ignore, hide a problem;* All faults can't be swept under the carpet.

Reach an understanding = *agreement;* They have reached an understanding on his admission.

Little understanding = *little ability to know;* People have little understanding of Greek.

Give an undertaking = *guarantee, pledge;* Antony gave an undertaking that he would return the goods.

Undervalue something = *underestimate the value;* His talents have been undervalued in his country.

Underworld = *world of crime;* He is a king of underworld.

Undiminished zeal = *not lessened, minimised;* Shell is still writing with undiminished zeal.

Undiplomatic move = *lacking tact, aim;* It was an undiplomatic move to reject the peace offer.

Undirected steps = *without aim, direction;* The undirected steps led to economic chaos.

Undisciplined masses = *uncontrolled;* You can't please undisciplined masses.

Undisclosed destination = *hidden, secret;* The fugitive has gone to an undisclosed destination.

Undreamed of = *never thought of;* Altaf is basking in undreamed of fame.

Undying desire = *permanent, everlasting;* Antony had an undying desire for beauty.

Unfit for = *without required qualities;* Simi is unfit for the post.

Unflinching courage = *without fear;* Dick faced the challenge with unflinching courage.

Unfold the mystery = *reveal, disclose;* Historians are unfolding the mystery of the pyramids.

Unforeseeable circumstances = *not anticipated, unseen;* You may face unforeseeable circumstances.

Unfounded fear = *baseless, untrue;* These are only unfounded fears.

Reach unanimity = *agreement;* We all reached unanimity on these steps.

Unanimous decision = *agreed by all;* It was a unanimous decision.

Unassuming = *kind, gentle;* He is an unassuming gentleman.

Uncalled for = *impolite, undesireable;*   Martin's action was uncalled for.

Underplay the role = *show as less important;*   You can't underplay his role in the team.

Undersized of one's age = *less than normal size;*   Paul is undersized of his age.

Under prepared plan = *incompletely prepared;*   This under prepared plan can't be implemented.

Leave unguarded = *leave without protection;*   The soldiers left the fort unguarded.

Unhampered progress = *without difficulty;*   Andy is making unhampered progress in life.

Unhealthy environment = *harmful;*   Poor people generally live in unhealthy environment.

Unheedful of = *pay no attention;*   Charlie was unheedful of the warning.

Unhistorical event = *not according to history;*   It is absolutely an unhistorical event.

Unholy alliance = *wicked relationship;*   They have formed an unholy alliance against us.

Uninfluential figure = *person with no influence;*   Hall is an uninfluential figure now.

Unintelligible to = *not to be understood;*   The sounds of animals are unintelligible to us.

Uninterested in = *unconcerned;*   The girls are uninterested in these games.

Uninviting place = *unattractive;*   This area is bleak and uninviting.

In unison = *simultaneously;* "We will also play," said the boys in unison.

In unison with = *in harmony;* All countries are in unison with us on this issue.

Universal phenomenon = *affecting the world;* Poverty is a universal phenomenon.

Unkind to someone = *rough, harsh;* Maggy is very unkind to me.

Unkind of = *inappropriate, improper;* It was unkind of Ken to abuse me.

Unknown to = *not familiar;* He is not unknown to me.

Unleash terror = *release;* Terrorists are unleashing a reign of terror.

Unlike to = *different from;* Barry is unlike his brother.

Unlimited measures = *without limits;* Natural resources are found in unlimited measures.

Unlikeable person = *not liked;* Indeed, Ian is an unlikeable person.

Unliveable place = *not to be lived in;* This is unliveable place for the children.

Unload the burden = *remove the burden;* Please unload the burden and feel relaxed.

Unlooked for = *unexpected, not seen;* In the college the boys found unlooked for joy and merriment.

Unlovable man = *not to be loved;* Hitler was an unlovable man for all civilised people of the world.

Unmake the law = *remove, reverse, annul;* The authorities have the full right to unmake the laws.

Unmanageable affair = *impossible to handle;* This is an unmanageable affair for us.

Unmanly act = *rude, improper;* The dictators are known for their unmanly acts.

Unmapped terrains = *unknown areas;* The explorers have explored many unmapped terrains.

Go unmarked = *unnoticed;* The player went unmarked and scored the goal.

Unmarketable goods = *not to be marketed;* These are unmarketable goods. We can't purchase them.

Unmatchable performance = *unequalled, unrivalled;* They gave unmatchable performance on the stage.

Corridor of uncertainty = *uncertain position;* Some players are now in the corridor of uncertainty.

Unmixed blessing = *have advantage and no disadvantage;* Good students have unmixed blessing.

Something is up = *some bad thing is afoot;* Be careful my friend, something is up.

Up against = *face difficulty;* He is up against a strong candidate.

Up on = *know, well informed;* The girls are up on the latest fashion.

Up and coming = *promising;* Sophia is an up and coming executive.

Uphill task = *tough, difficult;* To get a gold medal is an uphill task.

Have the upper hand = *gain advantage;* I have the upper hand over my rival.

Have no use for = *no need;* Henry has no use for this broken bat.

Of no use = *useless;* This pen is of no use to me.

A utopia = *unreal, impractical;* To think of a perfect world is a utopia.

Ultra virus = *beyond one's power;* The court decision is ultra virus.

Under the gun = *face criticism;* The coach is under the gun.

Under tight wraps = *under secrecy;* The dashing footballer is under tight wraps.

Umbilical link = *close, inseparable;* There is umbilical link between technology and business.

Unwavering faith = *strong;* I have unwavering faith in God.

The game is up = *end of something;* The game is up. You should accept defeat.

Up for = *available;* The book is up for sale.

What is up = *what is happening;* What is up with Ted?

To update something = *make more up to date;* Computer technology is updated everyday.

Upbeat about = *keen, cheerful;* Brian Lara is upbeat about his return to cricket.

Scoop up = *get;* He scooped up three gold medals for the country.

Under the belt = *victory one has won;* Ponting has many victories under his belt.

Urge someone on = *encourage;* Sam urges me on to do more work.

Vacillating mind = *wavering, fluctuating;* Dean has a fluctuating mind.

Leave a vacuum = *space;* His death has left a vacuum which can't be filled.

Take name in vain = *use a name in disrespect;* Bad boys take the name of elder people in vain.

Go in vain = *useless, unprofitable;* All my efforts went in vain.

Have no value = *know no worth of a thing;* Trevor has no value for this fine book.

Man of valour = *brave, courageous;* Richard the Lion was a man of valour.

Vamp up = *increase, improve;* A slight change in design will vamp up the value of this product.

A vampire = *people who prey on others;* There are some politicians who are vampires.

All is vanity = *worthless, useless;* What we see is all vanity.

Vantage point = *a place that gives good view;* Chief executives govern the business from vantage point.

Variety is the spice of life = *new and interesting experiences;* People go for new things because variety is the spice of life.

Draw a veil over = *hide, avoid to discuss;* Draw a veil over the circumstance of his death.

On velvet = *in prosperous condition;* Successful business houses are on velvet.

Venom and vitriol = *write devastatingly;* Jonathan Swift wrote with venom and vitriol.

Verbal duel = *heated exchange, hot words;* There was a verbal duel between John and Jim.

On the verge of = *very close to, near;* We are on the verge of defeat.

A vermin = *despicable people causing harm;* Bootleggers and drug barons are social vermins.

Verve and vigour = *energy, enthusiasm;* Humour adds verve and vigour to life.

Vexed question = *difficult question;* It is indeed a vexed question.

Vicious circle = *worse situation;* We are caught in a vicious circle of life.

In view = *aim or objective;* I have my work in view.

In view of = *as a result;* Ivan allowed me to go early in view of my health.

On view = *on display;* Many designs are on view.

With a view to = *with the object, aim;* Mona has come with a view to helping you.

Keep a vigil = *remain alert;* Roma's mother kept a night-long vigil.

A viper in one's bosom = *a person who betrays;* Ron is a viper in my bosom.

By virtue of = *because of ;* They completed the journey by virtue of his help.

Give voice to = *express;* Dick gave voice to his feelings.

With one voice = *in complete agreement;* We support him with one voice.

Volcanic eruption of something = *burst out with force;* There is a volcanic eruption of human follies.

Volte-face = *make a turnaround;* The government made a volte-face on economic policy.

Speak volumes about/for = *strong evidence;* This letter speaks volumes for her honesty.

Volumes of = *many;* Veenita gave volumes of figures in her support.

Vouch for = *assert, confirm;* I can vouch for his competency.

Vox populi = *opinion of majority;* We should respect vox populi.

Wafer thin = *very little;* They have wafer thin majority in parliament.

Wag one's tail = *show servility;* A greedy man wags his tail before a rich man.

How the world wags = *how the things are done;* Sam is confused and does not know how the world wags.

Wages of sin = *reward;* The wages of sin is death.

In wait = *observe, watch;* He is lying in wait for the robber.

Wait for = *stay till someone comes;* Please wait for me.

Wait on = *attend on someone;* He is waiting on the minister.

Play a waiting game = *refrain to act effectively;* The army is playing a waiting game outside enemy post.

Wake-up call = *a warning;* The price rise is a wake-up call for the government.

Walking dictionary = *man of knowledge;* Solomon is a walking dictionary.

Walk of life = *from different segments of society;* People from all walks of life come to the market.

Walk off with = *win;* Ken walked off with the trophy.

Walk-out = *go angrily;*   The members staged a walk-out.

Fight with back to the wall = *losing battle;*   The enemy is fighting with its back to the wall.

Off the wall = *crazy, eccentric;*   Mac was off the wall to hear this false story.

War of nerves = *war using psychological means;*   The countries fight a war of nerves.

On the wane = *become weak;*   His fame is on the wane.

Ward off = *stop, prevent;*   We put up resistance to ward off their advancement.

Warm up = *get interested in;*   Fred is warming up to his new job.

A warmonger = *advocate of war;*   Hitler was a warmonger.

On the warpath = *angry state;*   Our neighbours are on the warpath.

Washed out = *spoilt by rain;*   The match has been washed out.

Watch for = *look, find;*   We go to a park to watch for birds.

Be on the watch = *be careful;*   The snake is around so be on the watch.

Keep watch on = *be careful about someone;*   Keep watch on the pickpocket.

Water down = *dilute, make less forceful;*   He has watered down the proposals.

Of first water = *of great quality;*   He was an economist of first water.

A watershed = *a turning point;*   Darwin's theory is a watershed in the development of science.

Make waves = *make great impression;* Isaac Newton made waves as a scientist.

On the wavelength = *same ability, thinking;* Sarah and Claud are on the same wavelength.

Wax lyrical = *praise greatly;* She waxed lyrical about Tom's achievement.

Wax and wane = *undergo change;* Many ideas and concepts wax and wane in our life.

On one's way = *start one's journey;* Marx is on his way and will reach here soon.

Be on your way = *go away;* You are late and now be on your way.

Find a way out = *know a means to achieve the object;* I'll find a way out in spite of many hardships.

Give way to = *surrender or yield;* I will not give way to his threats.

Give way to = *lead to;* Ward's frustrations gave way to suicide.

Out of one's way = *make extra efforts;* She went out of her way to help me.

In some ways = *to some extent;* In some ways she is better than her brother.

In the family way = *pregnant;* Sophia is in the family way.

On the way out = *out of fashion;* Ths design is now on the way out.

Out of the way = *far away, remote;* His farm is out of the way.

Keep out of way = *avoid someone;* Shean keeps herself out of Tom's way.

The other way round = *opposite;* Here I find all things the other way round.

Ways and means = *methods;* The poor man has no ways and means to sustain himself.

Fall by the wayside = *fail to pursue the objective;* A few people achieve greatness, while others fall by the wayside.

The weak link = *weak point;* Fielding is the weak link in our team.

In wear = *in fashion;* Jeans are in wear.

Wear thin = *become less;* Alma's courage is now wearing thin.

Wear and tear = *damage;* This shirt is wear and tear free.

All weather = *good for all seasons;* These are all weather garments.

In all weathers = *in every weather;* This jacket can be worn in all weathers.

Make heavy weather = *unnecessary difficulty;* Dean made a heavy weather of this minor problem.

Under the weather = *unwell;* I can't go with you as I am under the weather.

Get weaving = *work fast;* My friend, it is time you should get weaving.

Drive a wedge = *separate things;* It is not Maggy's intention to drive a wedge between her friends.

Weed out = *remove, cut away;* Let us weed out corruption from society.

Throw one's weight behind = *use influence to support;* Ruth threw her weight behind Eva.

The weight of the world = *heavy responsibility;* Abner carries the weight of the world on his shoulders.

Silly as a wheel = *stupid, foolish;* William is as silly as a wheel.

Wheeling and dealing = *dubious dealings;* I have no idea of the wheeling and dealing of business world.

End with a whimper = *anticlimatic way;* He started with a bang but ended with a whimper.

Whip up = *create feelings;* The teacher tried to whip up Sam's interest in Physics.

Whipping boy = *punish someone for other's fault;* Pat is the whipping boy of the class.

Whispering campaign = *a rumour to damage reputation;* A whispering campaign is going on against the minister.

Clean as a whistle = *clear and clean;* The hotel was as clean as a whistle.

Black and white = *in writing;* Grace wants everything in black and white.

Bleed white = *take away all money and wealth;* The greedy man bled the old man white.

White-collar job = *office job;* Job wants only a white-collar job.

White elephant = *useless possession;* The three-bedroom home proved to be a white elephant for the lonely man.

As white as a lily = *absolutely white;* Ken's shirt is as white as a lily.

Show the white feather = *act cowardly;* When the fight started, Ronald showed the white feather.

White information = *correct and solid information;* All business houses want white information.

Whitewash something = *conceal mistake;* He whitewashed all the charges against him.

A whizz-kid = *an extremly successful young person;* Diana is a maths whizz-kid.

As a whole = *generally;* This medicine is very good for you as a whole.

A wild card = *uncertain and unpredictable;* Don't depend on Arthur. He is a wild card.

Wildcat strike = *sudden;* The workers have gone on a wildcat strike.

Will do = *suffice;* This book will do.

At will = *as one pleases;* You can leave the job at will.

With a will = *with energy and interest;* One should do a work with a will.

Wilt under pressure = *lose energy;* I will not wilt under pressure.

Win the day = *be successful;* Alice is working hard and will win the day finally.

Get wind of = *know something is going to happen;* Tony got the wind of his dismissal from job.

Sail close to the wind = *face disaster;* The lazy businessman is sailing close to the wind.

Throw to the wind = *neglect, pay no attention;* I threw all caution to the winds.

Wind down = *end, close;* The traders are now winding down their business.

Go out of the window = *disappear;*   Old fashions and trends are going out of the window.

Window of opportunity = *favourable opportunity;*   This organisation will give me a window of opportunity.

Window dressing = *misleading presentation;*   Remove poverty' is only a window dressing on the part of the government.

Good wine needs no bush = *good thing requires no publicity;*   Our product is excellent and a good wine needs no bush.

As easy as winking = *very easy;*   To solve this problem is as easy as winking.

In the wink of an eye = *quickly;*   My purse was taken away in the wink of an eye.

Winnow out = *find out;*   It is difficult to winnow out the cause of the problem.

Wipe out = *destroy;*   Poaching will wipe out many precious species from the world.

Wipe the slate clean = *forget past mistakes;*   Now we are good friends. Let us wipe the slate clean.

Go down to the wire = *result is decided at the last moment;*   The match is tough and will go to the wire.

Wish-wash = *weak, sentimental;*   His works are only wish-wash.

Wishy-washy = *feeble, weak;*   Our democracy is wishy-washy.

Scared out of wits = *frightened;*   I was scared out of my wits to see a tiger from close range.

Away with = *crazy, out;*   Derek is away with his head.

Be with someone = *support, agree;*   I am always with you.

Outwit someone = *deceive, cheat;*   In no way can you outwit me.

Wither away = *decay, decline;*   Plants without water wither away.

Keep the wolf from the door = *have money to avoid hunger;*   A poor man can hardly keep the wolf from the door.

Woman of letters = *a woman writer;*   The Bronte sisters were women of letters.

Woman of streets = *a prostitute;*   Woman of the streets generally operates at night.

No wonder = *not surprising;*   It is no wonder that this watch is the best.

One-day wonder = *of short interest;*   This show is only a one-day wonder.

Work wonders = *prove very useful;*   Ths medicine will work wonders.

Out of the woods = *out of danger;*   The team is out of the woods now.

Have a word = *speak to someone;*   I will have a word with Dora about you.

Man of his word = *keep one's promise;*   He is very honest and a man of his word.

Of few words = *brief, precise;*   She is a woman of few words.

Put into words = *express in speech or writing;*   They can't put their experience into words.

Take at word = *believe a person's word;* A child takes his parents at their word.

Work out = *understand;* I can't work out what you have written.

Get worked up = *excited, angry;* She got worked up to see a snake in her room.

At work = *doing something;* The electrician is at work.

In working condition = *in good shape;* My car is in working condition.

Work with clocklike precision = *accurately;* The engineers are working with clocklike precision.

Workaholic = *person who is fond of hard work;* Scientists are generally workaholics.

Worldly goods = *things one owns;* The rich people possess all worldly goods.

Worms one's way into = *slowly make ones way;* Shrewd politicians worm their way into the party.

Worn out = *look tired;* Martha looks worn out after a long journey.

Not to worry = *situation is not serious;* My friend, you need not to worry. You are out of danger.

Fear the worst = *think of an unpleasant situation;* As he was badly injured, I feared for the worst.

At someone's worst = *unpleasant state;* Nowadays my family is at its worst.

Wrap up = *finish, complete;* We wrapped up the Test series in style.

Wriggle out = *avoid by dishonest ways;* You have signed the agreement and now you can't wriggle out of it.

In writing = *give something in written form;* Please give me your statement in writing.

Writing is on the wall = *sign of danger;* The clouds of war are looming large and the writing is on the wall.

Get someone wrong = *to misunderstand a person;* Please don't get me wrong.

Go wrong = *enter bad ways;* You are going wrong, my friend.

In the wrong = *a person responsible for a mistake;* Luke is in the wrong.

On the wrong side = *disliked by someone;* Lynda is on the wrong side of her boss.

Walk off = *leave, resign;* He walked off the job.

Veiled warning = *hidden, secret;* It is a veiled warning to the workers.

In the wake of = *after, as a result;* The party is happy in the wake of their landslide victory.

Without no end = *always;* Good people help others without no end.

Wave a magic wand = *cast a spell, charm;* Zidane waves a magic wand and weaves soccer spell.

A new-wave product = *novel, new thing;* This car is a new-wave product.

Wait in the wings = *to be used at right time;* We have a number of executives waiting in the wings.

On the wing = *happy;* During Christmas, children are on the wing.

Under one's wing = *under care, control;*   The patient is under the wing of the doctor.

Nine days' wonder = *an attractive thing which is ignored later on;*   Some songs are only nine days' wonder.

Wool-gathering = *absent-minded;*   Have you gone wool-gathering?

Keep one's word = *fulfil one's promise;*   A truthful person keeps his word.

Take someone's word = *believe;*   We rarely take politician's word.

Work to perfection = *work nicely, completely;*   The management wants workers who work to perfection.

Workhorse = *a dependable person or machine;*   Canberra bombers were the workhorses of the Allied forces.

A world of difference = *very great;*   There is a world of difference between capitalism and communism.

Worlds apart = *very different;*   Churchill and Stalin were worlds apart.

X-rated = *bad, indecent;* He made a x-rated remark.

X-ray something = *examine something with x-rays;* All my belongings were x-rayed at the airport.

A yahoo = *a brute, nasty creature;* There are also some yahoos in our society.

By the yard = *in large quantity;* Football is inspiring western people by the yard.

Yardstick = *measurement;* Companies use different yardsticks to know one's performance.

Yearn for = *desire, a longing;* Children are yearning for wildlife.

On yellow alert = *a warning for a danger;* The river is rising and the people are on yellow alert.

Get a yellow card = *give a caution;* The player was shown a yellow card.

Yellow journalism = *exciting, sensational;* Many people now believe in yellow journalism.

Yeoman service = *give useful help;* Good leaders do yeoman service to the country.

Yesterday's man = *a man whose career is finished;* That politician is a yesterday's man.

Year in, year out = *regularly;* I stay in this hotel year in, year out.

Yield under pressure = *give up;* A good worker never yields under pressure.

Of yore = *of the past;* He told many stories of yore.

Be yourself = *in one's usual state;* Don't hide anything. Be yourself.

A zealot = *fanatical person;* Ezra is a zealot.

At one's zenith = *highest point;* Tom has reached the zenith of his career.

Zero in = *fix one's attention;* The police zeroed in on the murderer.

Full of zip = *very energetic;* These children are full of zip.

Zoom off = *go or move very fast;* The plane zoomed off.

Sentence Correction for admission to Foreign Universities

—A.P. Sharma

GMAT, GRE & TOEFL

✓ This booklet is intended to teach how to reduce the errors that occur in the Sentence Correction Test for Admission to Foreign Universities.

✓ It also teaches us how to locate the various types of errors in sentences.

✓ The basic rules of Grammar have been explained briefly and systematically.

✓ The examples and exercises given in this booklet will make you familiar with the different types of questions and provide you with sufficient practice to use the different techniques for answering each type of question.

✓ There is also a practice test to evaluate your progress and make you perfect.

Pages: 168 • Price: Rs. 80/-

Words & Phrases that carry
Uncommon Meanings

—Dr. A.P. Sharma

The book aims to display uncommon expressions that look common but are uncommon in usage and meaning. The uncommon expressions are interwoven within he conversations fitted into suitable situations. Dialogues containing common and uncommon expressions, phrases and idioms are developed in a most fascinating style displaying a rich vocabulary and appropriate language that provides a modern touch. In this respect, the reader will have a face chance to experience varied and trying situations during different sets of conversations.

The book not only provides new vistas of vision as regards learning how to converse with the people, but also extends before the reader new sets of situations knitted in dialogues enabling one to enrich his/her linguistic capabilities.

Pages: 136 • Price: Rs. 72/-